"Wonderful work... So full of nugg
continuously,"
Victor Chan, co-founder with F.....
The Dalai Lama Center for Peace And Education.

"I was delighted... I agree completey with your analysis of both the cause
and solution to our problems,"
David Suzuki.

"I have to read it four or times more; there is so much wisdom in it,"
Susan Ruzic, Vice President,
B.C. Teachers for Peace And Global Education.

"... the global issues that exist today were neither created overnight, nor
by some government, nor by some corporation, nor by some magical source;
they were created by the likes of you and me, one drop at a time. It will take
you and me to resolve them ..."

This first book by Pummy Kaur contains many unique insights and perspectives, and offers simple, highly effective, individual solutions to global problems. Solutions that are congruent with principles gleaned from the life and work of Gandhi; such as, simplicity, seva (service), self-sufficiency, courage, and compassion.

This very timely book clearly and succinctly demonstrates that current global problems are reversible within our lifetimes, without government, business, industry or financial sector assistance. All that is needed is the active, individual will of the Western Minded to stop being so very lazy, so very addicted to convenience, and so very brainwashed by the Trash Media.

With many people worldwide feeling hopeless, helpless and disillusioned with the ability of any one person to do anything about the big problems in our global village, a new author has arrived to guide us through the maze. Kaur shows us the links between the individual actions of the Western Minded and the planet wide effects that follow. Effects that include; global warming, climate change, the rates of extinction of species and cultures, the amassment of nuclear weapons, the illegal occupations and wars, the violence against the feminine, the epidemics of diseases, growing religious fundamentalist/neo-conservative movements, bioengineering, the excessive controls granted to international financial institutions and the deliberate perpetuation by them of the poverty of nations, the rights of most multi-national corporations now superceding those of most sovereign nations, the enforced mal-development of the Majority World, and the lethal burdens now placed upon the natural systems of our Earth's biosphere by the lifestyles of the Western Minded.

Several features make this book unique. One of the most notable features is that much of the responsibility is placed squarely on all our collective shoulders for the creation, and also the solving of global problems. In a simple, yet passionate style of a genuine educator, this work connects the dots between global problems and our individual choices. Kaur provides rationale, and also concrete, easy solutions to very complex, global problems.

This book challenges the Western Minded of all ages, races, genders, faiths, locations, trades, professions, colours, and nationalities to examine their own individual complicity in global problems. And, further to that, it also inspires educated, selfless, future conscious, compassionate individual actions.

Order this book online at www.trafford.com/07-0084
or email orders@trafford.com

Most Trafford titles are also available at major online book retailers.

Note for Librarians: A cataloguing record for this book is available from Library and Archives Canada at www.collectionscanada.ca/amicus/index-e.html

Printed in Victoria, BC, Canada.

ISBN: 978-1-4251-1685-9

We at Trafford believe that it is the responsibility of us all, as both individuals and corporations, to make choices that are environmentally and socially sound. You, in turn, are supporting this responsible conduct each time you purchase a Trafford book, or make use of our publishing services. To find out how you are helping, please visit www.trafford.com/responsiblepublishing.html

Our mission is to efficiently provide the world's finest, most comprehensive book publishing service, enabling every author to experience success. To find out how to publish your book, your way, and have it available worldwide, visit us online at www.trafford.com/10510

www.trafford.com

North America & international
toll-free: 1 888 232 4444 (USA & Canada)
phone: 250 383 6864 ♦ fax: 250 383 6804
email: info@trafford.com

The United Kingdom & Europe
phone: +44 (0)1865 722 113 ♦ local rate: 0845 230 9601
facsimile: +44 (0)1865 722 868 ♦ email: info.uk@trafford.com

10 9 8 7 6 5 4

What Would Gandhi Do?

K.I.S.S.:
Keep It Simple Solutions
To Global Problems
by Pummy Kaur

10% of profits to be donated to **His Holiness The Dalai Lama** Center for Peace Education in British Columbia, Canada

Contents

Dedication

This work of love is dedicated to my grandmother, Prem Kaur, whose first name translates to " love ", and whose last name, carrying centuries of female, pre-colonial identity, loosely translates into "princess, with the heart of a lioness". She loved me unconditionally, nurtured me, and taught me about a life of seva (service) and compassion. I wish she were here now.

It is also dedicated to my three children Hadley, Kipling, and Cadence, and to the thousands of children I have taught; for, it is they who taught me what it means to be human in the most profound sense of the word. Also, it was they who taught me how to use a computer so that I could write this first of my books that have been percolating for many years.

Lastly it is dedicated to the man who said in a few words what every religion has hoped to achieve with volumes of literature.

"WE MUST BE THE CHANGE WE WISH TO SEE IN THE WORLD ",

Mohandas K Gandhi (pronounced like "Khan – thee" with a "G", not like "candy" with a "G").

Acknowledgements

How can one ever offer thanks for all that transpired in one's life leading to the present moment? It is a daunting task to acknowledge all those that contributed to this work. All that I know, and all that I am are a direct result of everything I have experienced, the horrific and the blessed. Foremost, I am grateful to the Divine Beloved for all the people, places and experiences that have given me the insights shared in this work.

My daughters, Hadley and Cadence, have my gratitude for their continuous support, as does my son, Kipling, for being my technological guide as I learned to navigate the world of a laptop. An affectionate thanks goes to my "sister-out-law" Jackie Beaurivage, and to my sister-in-law Xu Xiao Bo, for holding my hand through the ordeal of cancer and its cure these last six months, and for always believing in my abilities to write this book.

Thank you Gudrun Howard for making me look good by editing, and enhancing the manuscript, and for all the other works of mine that you have edited previously. Thanks to Bill Piket for valuable input, and Kevin Amboe for very generous technical support. Much gratitude goes to Jack Layton for reading, commenting on, and supporting this venture. Thank you Kimberly McMillan for finding a publisher for me. Thank you to everyone at Trafford Publishing especially Bill Mitchell.

THE UNIVERSAL DECLARATION OF RIGHTS AND RESPONSIBILITIES OF DEPENDENCE

We, the people, of planet Earth, and all its creatures, plants, bodies of water, lands, and air within the living biosphere, as well as it's Sun, Solar System, Galaxy, Universe, the Cosmos and Time, and the Source of all these, are utterly and completely dependent upon each other for our existence. In our utter dependence upon all that is in the space-time continuum we humans have rights and responsibilities to all else that exists, hereafter called "Others".

We have the right to have our basic physiological needs met, and we have the responsibility to ensure we not deprive Others of what is essential for their physiological make up.

We have the right to live in safety, and we have the responsibility to ensure our actions do not diminish the safety of Others.

We have the right to the comforts of community, and we have the responsibility to let the communities of Others be as they see fit.

We have the right to hold ourselves in good esteem, and we have the responsibility to also hold all Others in equal or higher esteem.

We have the right to self actualize, and we have the twin responsibilities of ensuring we raise our children in ways that will ensure greater self actualization for our species, and of not interfering with the self actualization of Others.

We, the people of Planet Earth dedicate ourselves to protecting the life of all that exists, for without Existence there is no "We the people." We, the people, of planet Earth dedicate ourselves self consciously to exercising all of our rights with passion for peace, justice and equity for ourselves. We dedicate ourselves selflessly with passion and compassion to all the concomitant responsibilities that accompany these rights of complete and utter dependence.

This author feels much gratitude to Abraham Maslow for the inspiration provided with his hierarchy of human needs, and hopes this book provides people with enough knowledge, actions and inspiration to live by this declaration of DEpendence.

CHAPTER ONE:
FOR THE RECORD

Life is life in a certain way.
Make it funny in a day,
Make it creative or may,
Be kind, thankful and true.
Then life will be good to you.
Many things make life nice.
Nature and towns are wonderful things.
I like dolphins and whales,
You might just like me.
Life is the best, like me and you.
So, make it nice in your paradise.
                    T. Dashwood, age 7

Unfamiliar terminology, or terminology having differently understood meaning may be used in this work. The following is a list to clarify the author's use of certain terminology.

1 **B.C.E.** – Before the Common Era, instead of B.C., even though it refers to the same benchmark for dating, it eliminates religious reference, and thus is more inclusive.

2 **Big B.S.** – short hand for "Big Box Stores", selling goods manufactured by minors in sweatshops devoid of safety, environmental or labour standards.

3 **C.E.**- Common Era, instead of A.D., which is religion based and not inclusive of the majority of humanity who are not of that religion.

4 **COSMOS** – refers to the sum of all that there is, which includes our universe, and perhaps multiple others, as well as the Source of all that there is.

5 **E.W.1.and E.W.2** – refer to the first and second European Wars, which are erroneously known as W.W.1 and W.W.2., for they were wars amongst the European countries over control of the resources of the invaded colonies.

6 **FIRST PEOPLES, INDIGENOUS, NATIVE, FIRST NATIONS, TRIBAL, ABORIGINAL**– refer to the pre-colonial peoples, whose ancient oral traditions or texts place them on given lands centuries prior to colonization.

7 **INDIAN** – refers to people of origin in the Indian sub-continent. East Indian and West Indian are highly derogatory term created by the colonizers to differentiate between the Caribbean Islands Indian slaves from India and the Pacific Island Indian slaves. Hence, the terms East and West Indies were created, in geographic relation to Europe, to name mil-

lions of people whose centuries old identities existed prior to colonization.

8   **JI** (pronounced "GEE")– is a term used in India to show respect for elders and for some titles regardless of age. It is considered ill mannered to address an elder by name only without the "ji" following.

9   **MAJORITY WORLD** – this is a non-judgmental, based in fact, reference to what is called the Third World or the Developing World in an arbitrary, value laden ranking.

10   **MIND** – a psycho-spiritual non-local entity where awareness seems to occur, and not to be confused with the brain located in the skull, which is a physical entity.

11   **MINORITY WORLD** – the 20% of the world that comprises most of the Western Minded, arrogantly referred to as The First World.

12   **NON-HUMAN ANIMALS** – refers to all the other creatures, while recognizing humans are only one amongst millions of animal species.

13   **STUFF** – is used to refer to all the material goods we acquire that are not essential for wellbeing or survival.

14   **USONIAN** – coined by Buckminster Fuller, refers to citizens of the U.S.A., who are only one of the many groups occupying the Americas, stretching from the southern tip of S. America, through Central America and The Caribbean, and to the northern tip of N. America.

15   **UNIVERSE** – refers to the one universe that we commonly believe is the home of our solar system.

16 **UNIVERSAL "THEY "**– refers to the "they" to which people often point in suggesting who should be responsible for solving any problems.

17 **WESTERN MIND** – an entire chapter follows to explain this term, and it refers to the mind of many of the 20% named above as The Minority World.

18 **WHOLE FOODS** – are foods and drinks that have either not been processed at all, such as produce, whole grains, pulses, range fed livestock, water, and organic tea leaves, or foods that have been minimally processed such as whole grain and live grain breads, and some dairy products.

19 **WORLD** – is used to refer to the people of this planet, as differentiated from the planet itself, referred to as Earth.

CHAPTER TWO:

WHY?

Watch over me,
Hold your hand before me in protection.
Stand before me and arise as my protector
Do my commands as I do your bidding.
Let no harm befall me from the air as I breathe,
From the rain as it falls, from the Thunders as they strike,
From below the plants, from the trees under which water flows.
Dewdrops and pollen may I enjoy.
With these may it be beautiful before me.
With these may it be beautiful behind me.
All is beautiful again, all is restored in beauty.
                              A Navajo Prayer

Dear Reader,

This book has been in the making for about twenty years, the impetus for finally writing it coming while recovering from breast cancer. I have realized there is no time like the present for doing what is in one's heart. This book is not just about peace, nor about human rights, nor about any one of the thousand social injustice issues that plague humanity today. It is, in fact, about all of them. It is about our individual complicity in these issues. It is about highly effective individual, simple solutions to complex, global issues.

Mahatma Gandhi lived simply, yet he addressed the most serious, complex problems facing India: colonial brutality, Indian sovereignty, women's rights, equity for all, peaceful conflict resolution, and so much more. He inspired Martin Luther King, Nelson Mandela, Mother Theresa, and is frequently quoted by celebrities, the famous, and our elected officials worldwide. Gandhi ji held no title, he was elected to nothing, he owned nothing, and yet he freed an entire nation from one hundred and fifty years of barbaric occupation. This work is not directly about him. It is about solutions that would be consistent with his beliefs about living in ways that would positively address current global issues.

The issues that exist today were neither created overnight, nor by some government, nor by some corporation, nor by some other magical source; they were created by the likes of you and me, one drop at a time. It will take you and me to resolve them. The intent of this work is to shed some light on just how individual complicity is involved in global issues; to offer ways of becoming the change we wish to see; and, to become the change agents who model the desired behaviors, attitudes and skills.

It is imperative for us to become effective citizens of the world, not just of our own hometowns. We are linked to the lives of people in every part of the world. Our coffee comes from South America, our sugar from the Philippines, our cocoa from Ghana, our rum from Jamaica, our wine from France, our garments from China, our rugs from Pakistan, our electronics from Japan, our tobacco from The Caribbean, our paper from the few remaining ancient rainforests, our peanuts from Africa, our rice from S. E. Asia, our furniture from Scandinavia, our oil from the Middle East, our spices from India, our vanilla from Mexico, our opium from Afghanistan, our cars from Korea, our fruit from the tropics, our fashions from Europe, our cigars from Cuba, our weapons of mass destruction from the U.S.A., our homophobia and intolerances from Vatican City, and even our national populations are made up of international immigrants, except for a few descendents of the First Peoples. Due to our inextricable interdependence upon each other, now we must become more aware of how our individual lives effect the global welfare of all, including all other species, and the living biosphere that sustains all of our lives. **To live as a responsible member of the biosphere is to be a good global citizen.**

The single biggest threat to all nations comes from a single nation with a long history of rogue administrations. The people of most nations have abdicated their responsibilities to their own national sovereignties; they have allowed a single rogue nation the power to control planetary resources, information, and to amass the largest stockpile of nuclear, biological and chemical W.M.D. ever. Our habits of excessive consumption and disposal of all the planet's resources give impetus to these rogue administrations to control these resources, and thereby controlling wealth and power. That is, whoever controls the resources, controls the wealth and power of the world.

Gandhi ji knew the power of self-sufficiency when he initiated the salt march, and that soon lead to India's freedom. We can follow this example of self-sufficiency and make this rogue nation redundant, irrelevant and powerless. As long as we continue our excessive consumption of the resources of this planet, the rogue administrations of the U.S.A. will continue to flourish. It is our greed that is at the root of wars. Our governments, financial institutions, and the business sectors have no incentive to take a stand against the administrations of the U.S.A., or it's client states. This work offers the reader several means by which to regain national sovereignty, and deprive these rogue administrations of the U.S.A. of their reason to control resources, and to control the world. This situation is not too dissimilar from the power of a drug pusher over an addict; this power to control and continue wealth amassment can last only as long as one is addicted. Kick the habit, and kick the butt of the pusher right out of usefulness and relevancy.

I have been practicing and preaching good global citizenship using my THREE Rs for a few decades, and I believe these ought to be the baseline for what it means to be an educated human, a good global citizen.

The Global Three RS:
RESPECT, RESTORE AND REVERE ALL OF LIFE.

Having done this work in international seminars, teacher training sessions, publishing many articles, creating public school and Sunday School curricula, teaching all levels from pre-school to senior citizens in four countries, visiting schools in dozens more, guest lecturing at universities, giving many speeches on personal solutions to global issues, and trying to be the change I wish to see, it has been the latter that has been so very, very hard to do in comparison. I still struggle with it daily. However, I am inspired to carry on when I remember that Gandhi ji also said that no matter how insignificant an act may seem to be, what is most important is that you do it, with the best of intentions. Furthermore, what if I might be the hundredth monkey?* Or what if I influence

---

* "The Hundredth Monkey" was coined after a group of scientists had been studying monkeys on a remote island. A lone, young female monkey began to wash fallen fruit before eating it. She taught her mother, and then others on the island quickly learned it. Soon monkeys on neighbouring islands began to do it, without ever having had contact with the first mentioned island.

The Hundredth Monkey concept refers to the phenomenon of all members of a species "getting it", without there having been any empirical observation of any-

someone who becomes the hundredth monkey. So, I feel compelled to carry on with those two inspirations in my heart.

You will find a little intellectual and emotional rage in this work. Yes, I am outraged at the extent of the horrors the human race inflicts upon the most innocent, the most vulnerable, and the most precious; the children of the world. I am outraged by the heartlessness, and chosen blindness of the comfortable wealthy. I am outraged at the cultural genocide of the few who remain with answers for humanity. I am outraged that women and girls suffer needlessly. I am outraged at the hypocrisy of religious leaders. I am outraged at the invasion and devastation of Tibet, which has the most loving and peaceful people of all nations. I am outraged that the USonians saw fit to murder innocent Iraqi civilians over oil rich Kuwait, and do nothing to protect spirit rich Tibetans. I am outraged that the Western Minded stand witness to all this and do absolutely nothing! I would like to scream, "Stop it you heartless, lazy, evil, immature bastards!" but that would be very contrary to the principles by which I am aspiring, and daily struggling, to live.

"IF YOU'RE NOT OUTRAGED, YOU ARE NOT PAYING ATTENTION."
This was seen on a bumper sticker.

You will not find every thought and concept presented referenced and sourced. That would not only be counter-productive to keeping it simple, but also because that is a custom of the very mind that I warn against in this work. To this mind it is necessary to appeal to some external authority for validation, allowing no place for independent, original or inspired thought. I do not lack the necessary skills to reference my work. I have the alphabet soup I could attach to my name. However, as an educator I promote education well before schooling. I would like to believe that I am

---

thing having been passed on amongst the members. There is some magical number at which critical mass is reached and all members "get it". This number is referred to as The Hundredth Monkey.

on the road to becoming well educated, recovering from having had excessive schooling. What I offer the reader here is some of my education; distilled, readable, accessible and applicable to the lives of the vast majority who are not academicians. I have included a list of the sources that have most influenced me. My assertions can easily be checked by those so inclined; however, verifying original thought can be challenging when there is no precedence to which to appeal.

There will be those amongst the readers who will dismiss the arguments presented because it is too difficult to admit one's complicity and continue doing nothing about it.

Healing can only begin when one first acknowledges that there is dis-ease.

There will be others who will fail to act because they perceive one person's actions will amount to nothing.

Current issues are the cumulative result of at least five hundred years of individual little actions.

There are those who will expend large amounts of energy finding excuses for why the recommended solutions won't work.

It is more beneficial to search for effective creative solutions and make them work than it is to search for validating excuses for inaction.

There will be others who will assert that it is impossible for the poor to implement the solutions.

It is not only that the poor do not have many choices in how to survive, but also this work is not written for the poor to assimilate into their lives; it is written for the comfortable Western Minded. However, I would recommend reading it to the Western Minded Wanna-Bes.

There already are those who lay blame on the populations of China, India and Africa amongst others, for what they are expected to do to the future of the planet by adopting Western Minded lifestyles. And furthermore, these same people insist that we should do something to stop them.

Firstly, it is not China, India, Africa or any other Majority World country that has created the lethal conditions that already exist today. Secondly, if it is wrong for them to harm the planet, then why is it appropriate for us to do so?

There will be more still who will lay blame on governments, businesses, industry, manufacturers, and every thing and everyone else, the Universal "They", for having failed to do the right thing.

The leaders will begin to follow when the people begin to lead by first making changes in their own lives. Industries and businesses will change when there is no longer any demand or tolerance for their unnecessary products and services.

Many others will place their faith in science and technology to solve the problems.

Firstly, it has been the use of science and technology without ethics that has created many of the problems. We currently have all the technology we need to eradicate all the human created problems. What we lack is leadership with an internal moral compass in both our homes and nations. Furthermore, there is no financial incentive in removing the supply of problems serviced by somebody's industry.

The leaders of industries, governments, churches, and financial institutions will protest that my claims are unsupported, unreferenced, female ranting.

I would welcome being made into a fool and proven wrong, by the

research of mutually acceptable, disinterested third parties. It would be a grand day for all of Life if the leaders of our governments, religions, businesses, and financial institutions were proven to be a balance of responsible capitalism and effective socialism.

Unfortunately there will be those who will become so enraged that they will not read beyond whatever point enraged them, and will instead hurl abuses at the author.

It is often the case that if the reflection is unpleasing when a mirror is held up, it is the holder of the mirror that becomes the target of the anger. Queen Gertrude did, indeed, protest too much.

Of course, there will be those who will point with glee at the author's shortcomings in implementing all the recommendations, declaring her to be a hypocrite with no credibility, thereby dismissing her entire message.

Not only are the author's shortcomings irrelevant, for it is the message that is most significant, but also, it would be of greater service to humanity to emulate the plethora of things being done right, rather than to use the few in need of more effort, as an excuse for inaction.

And then, finally, there are those few who, either already are, or will be the courageous souls awakening and becoming the messengers by example.

I applaud them and thank them on behalf of my own three adored children, and all the world's children alive today, tomorrow and for at least the next seven generations. Of these brave souls I ask, please give copies of this book to the people who most need to read it, and I fear, will be the least likely to do so.

We, the baby boomer yuppies and our puppies, are the first generations in the history of humanity to leave this planet and the Life on it in worse shape than when we found it, in every way conceivable. It is time to acknowledge this and fix it, if we want there to be future generations. Or not! It really does not matter in the long run. We are destined to become extinct in any event, individually, and as a species. The average life span of extinct species has been about 100,000 years, and the human intellect evolved enough to develop the infrastructures of a civilization just about that long ago. This Universe does not need us to survive; we desperately need it, and once extinct, we will be missed by absolutely nothing. It is up to us how we chose to go: in a brutal, quick, self-inflicted end, taking down many more innocent species with us, or slowly, with dignity, having given meaning to our existence.

If Life and the living of it on this planet do matter then it really matters how we choose to live. We can choose to live with purpose and nobility, as if Life really matters! Or, we can carry on in this self-destruct mode. Hope is never futile. Dreams are not just fantasy. We can dream any new dreams of how we want to turn out as a species, when we finally grow up. We can let our dreams be the guides, and use the power of hope to propel us to act now and stop laying blame on governments, corporations, other nations, other cultures, or our religious institutions. When we point a finger of blame, we need to look at where the other three are pointing.

In solidarity for peace and justice,
Pummy Kaur,
British Columbia, Canada
July 2006, C.E.

"My heart is moved by all I can not save;
So much has been destroyed
I have to cast my lot with those who, age after age,
Perversely, with no extraordinary power,
Reconstitute the world."
> *Adrienne Rice*

CHAPTER THREE:
GANDHIAN PRINCIPLES

No bars are set too close, no mesh too fine,
To keep me from the eagle and the lion,
Whom keepers feed that I may freely dine.
This goes to show that if you have the wit
To be small, common, cute and live on shit,
Though the cage fret kings, you may make free with it.

The Sparrow in the Zoo, H. Nemerov

There are large volumes of literature about Gandhi ji, and the reader has easy access to most of them. What follows is not more about Gandhi ji, but about principles he espoused that have inspired this author, in how to live, and also in selecting the most significant content for this work.

GUIDING PRINCIPLES:

1   *Give gratitude daily.*

2   *Have silence regularly.*

3   *Be humble at all times.*

4   *Practice the spiritual essence of one's own faith.*

5   *Keep it simple.*

6   *Be respectful.*

7   *Be self sufficient and self controlled.*

8   *Practice non-violence in thoughts, words and deed, for it is the weapon of the strong.*

9   *Honour the opponent, never humiliate.*

10   *Proactively counter the seven blunders that lead to violence;*

~ *wealth without work,*   ~ *knowledge without character,*

~ *commerce without morality,*   ~ *science without humanity,*

~ *worship without sacrifice,*   ~ *politics without principles.*

~ *pleasure without conscience,*

11   *Just do it, no matter how insignificant, with good intentions.*

12   *Reflect on the impact of decisions on the least amongst us, especially on children.*

13   *Improve one's self in body, thinking and soul.*

14   *Satisfaction lies in the effort; full effort is full victory.*

15   *Use personal calamities for self-improvement.*

16   *TRUTH is what the voice within tells, LOVE is the other side of the same coin.*

17   *Pursuit of TRUTH/LOVE is the key to true health and wellbeing.*

18   *Act fearlessly upon what one believes is right.*

19   *Perform seva without an eye on any results.*

20   *Be the change you want to see in the world.*

CHAPTER FOUR:

THE BIG PICTURE

To see the world in a Grain of Sand,
And heaven in a Wild Flower,
Hold Infinity in the palm of your hand,
And eternity in an hour.
            William Blake

Religious and scientific creation myths worldwide have one fundamental feature in common; they all believe the entire cosmos has its origins in one source. Religious myths generally assert the source to be an all-powerful male being, and the science myth asserts it to be a single event before space-time. Spiritual and philosophical traditions such as Wicca, Buddhism and Confucian thought generally remain silent on the issue. Further to that, western science has recently confirmed the ancient beliefs of the pre-colonial peoples of Earth, that everything is connected.

Over the last century quantum science has not only verified that all that exist in our physical reality is in fact only energy, manifest in trillions of forms, but also that every manifestation effects every other one, regardless of distance, and perhaps even time. These things were known to our ancients for centuries, and are now being validated by the most advanced scientific methods we have. The most commonly known ancient teaching about the interconnectedness of all is that of Indra's Web in Hinduism, more recent is that of The Web of Life by Chief Seattle, and the most recently offered is by quantum physicists, including Einstein, Bohr, Heisenberg, and Capra.

It matters not which myth one believes, what matters is that we come to realize we are all children of a common parent. We share ancestry with every grain of sand, every creature, every plant, every drop of water, every galaxy in every universe. Everything that has ever existed, or ever happened any where in the Universe, or will exist or happen, influences everything through interconnection and interdependence of the energy that is the fundamental building block of all that appears to exist in space-time.

These ideas can seem too farfetched to be true. However, consider this. If they are true, then how we each live has a profound impact on everything else. There is simply too much scientific evidence to deny they are true. There is simply too much at stake to live as if they were false. Unfortunately the latter is what we have been doing and the current situation is looking very bleak. It is bleak for all, without regard to socio-economic standing, or geographic location, or culture, or anything else. Nowhere on this planet is anyone safe from nuclear fallout. Nowhere on this planet is anyone safe from the Sun's ultraviolet radiation. Nowhere on this planet is anyone safe from air, land and water pollution. Nowhere on this planet is anyone safe from epidemics such as H.I.V./A.I.D.S.. Nowhere on this planet is anyone safe from the newly, human created epidemic of extreme weather, and the not-so-natural natural disasters. At present there is no bank account large enough, no mansion grand enough, no island remote enough, no current faith system strong enough to protect the human race from itself.

We have more gross poverty than ever before in history. We have had more deaths due to war since the end of the last large scale European war than we had in both the European wars combined. The global rates of the following have risen to unprecedented gross numbers: homelessness, malnutrition, infant mortality, abuse of females, species extinction, cancer, incarcerations, executions, desertification, deforestation, climate changes, environmental and social pollutants, union busting, fundamentalism, natural resource depletion, monoculture-ism, drug trade and trafficking, militarization, nuclear waste accumulation, deaths from preventable diseases, and slavery, to name only the major ones.

None of these horrors appeared unbid out of thin air; we, the human race, created them. They are all interconnected and are primarily the result of the lifestyles of The Western Minded, conceived just prior to colonization, given birth during colonial times and now thriving in neo-colonization. If the reader can learn to accept the interconnected nature of all in the Cosmos and begin to act with more awareness, then we can begin to see an end to the bleak future that no one can escape at present. The major portion of this work is devoted to raising awareness, to making connections amongst seemingly disparate phenomena, and recommending simple actions we can all take to eradicate the bleak future that faces all of humanity if nothing is done. We created this and we can undo it, if the spirit is willing. Will your-self to just do it.

CHAPTER FIVE:

THE WESTERN MIND

So. The game was worth the candle,
Was the candle worth the cake?
Now you have it and you eat it.
Does it make your belly ache?
                    Jane King

The following is a highly abridged, somewhat biased, very generalized version of one perspective on a history of European colonization. The intention is not to dwell on debate over differing points of view, but to lead the reader through a long series of complex events in a few paragraphs in order to aid the reader in understanding aspects of today's issues. For a more thorough understanding of this history the reader is referred to any one of hundreds of sources on the subject at their public library, not just what is found on the Internet. The reader is cautioned to select sources from a variety of points of view. Any one source contains the biases of the author, including this work. So, consider a few perspectives before arriving at your conclusions. **No one source is an authority on anything!!!** It is great folly to believe otherwise.

There is evidence that even in prehistoric times there was friction amongst differing groups. There is ample evidence that invasions and occupations happened before the start of European colonization. However, the difference is that the latter effected nearly every nation adversely and the effects of the devastation in its wake are still with us. Consequently the following version of history focuses on that only.

Until about 1450 C.E. people lived in relatively isolated, harmonious groups, creating ways of life that were rooted in their geography. Some Indigenous Peoples remained the most isolated into the recent past, and developed some of the most ecologically, socially and spiritually sound cultural practices. Then came a time of great confusion for the peoples of Europe. Their religious beliefs were shattered by the discovery that the Earth was not the center of the Universe. When their adventurers returned with tales of other ways of living, and knowledge from other cultures that far exceeded their own cultural understandings, they were despondent. It was during this time of confusion that enormous atrocities were committed on anyone not fitting the image of their god. An estimated ten to sixty million women were executed in the first gender-based holocaust, euphemistically called The Witch Burnings. Hundreds of millions of Indigenous (nearly eighty million in The Americas alone) and people of colour were murdered in the Holocaust of Colonization. Colonization was the first period of Western Minded invasion, occupation, exploitation, and devastation of ancient cultures that had predated Western civilization by centuries.

Within a very short period after the onset of colonization nearly every nation on Earth had been occupied by one of a handful of European nations. Every effort was made by these invaders to enslave the local populations into serving the need of the invaders, exploiting natural resources, including the honours of the women and girls, and the strong young bodies of males for defending the invaders. All this was done to secure a position of power relative to other European nations. All the lands were exploited and plundered using the indentured labour of the innocent. What once was land that supported entire cultures became land for crops for European consumption and trade. Crops such as sugar, coffee, tea, cocoa, tobacco and peanuts replaced the multitude of crops that supported the needs of those now exploited. Since cultural identity was originally rooted in one's geography the dramatic changes in the land and vegetation, and the changes brought about by centuries of cruel abuses by the invaders, resulted in the rise of many, many dysfunctional cultures over successive generations.

The atrocities committed by the invaders were justified in many ways. Their belief system had taught them they were the ones chosen to have dominion over all the Earth, and that people of other faiths and colours were not really human. Often the invaders were funded by their monarchs and religious institutions, and were handsomely rewarded for annihilating entire villages of women, children, the elderly and the infirm. Shamelessly, even today, some have the audacity to describe magnanimity of the invaders as having been beneficial to the invaded peoples. For instance, it has been said frequently that India should be grateful to the invaders for what was done for Indians, such as the railways, schools, democracy and the English language.

The railways were only built to provide a more expedient means of transporting Indian resources to the ocean ports for shipment to England. India had its own educational systems that had successfully transmitted education to its various cultures for centuries before the invaders brought their religious indoctrination in the form of schooling. Democracy? When the invaders were finally removed from the lands they had illegally occupied they found insidious ways of leaving behind sympathizers in places of control. Thus the countries continued to serve the needs of the invaders, a situation not unlike the recent and current occupations of several Majority World countries by the USonians. As for giving the English language to the colonized, India had the oldest, most sophisticated written language, Sanskrit, and dozens of it's own languages centuries before the last physical occupation. One such language, Hindi, is the third most frequently spoken language in the world, and joins Mandarin, Cantonese, Spanish, Bengali in being spoken by more than the English language is. However, English has given the world a more commonly recognized language; as a result of colonization, not as a result of any inherent superiority of the language.

The points being made are that the generosity of the invaders had little to do with human decency and compassion, and had everything to do with serving only the masters. The interruption to the natural evolution of world cultures resulted in the devastation of families, tribes, and entire nations. All this havoc was wreaked while the peoples of Europe enjoyed the riches stolen from around the world. Average Europeans were oblivious to their own complicity in these holocausts of executions, murder and slavery of millions, of the ravaging of entire counties, or any of the other atrocities. The average citizen was content with the riches she or he consumed, be they silks, coffee, spices, tea or the site of the crown jewels, mostly robbed from other countries.

This is what I call the colonial mind, a precursor to the Western mind. A mind that is too self-absorbed for whatever reason to be aware of the misery caused to others through its own actions, beliefs and attitudes.

This situation continued until the first European War (E.W. 1), which is erroneously called the First World War. It was a war amongst European nations over the control of colonized nations and their resources. Of course the colonized were forced to fight in the wars for the glory of their masters. This became much more true of the second European War (E.W. 2). Millions of lives were lost in battle and millions of lives were devastated. But no leaders lost their lives, and they knowingly mislead their electorate and troops about the reasons for going to war, referring to them as being altruistic and philosophical. Altruism was not the case then, and blatantly more obvious, it is not the case now!

One only need look at the historical records to note when invaded nations started the rumblings for independence. Many began to work for independence just prior to E.W. 1. The rumblings became visible conflicts by E.W.2, resulting in most nations gaining their independence soon thereafter. Most of the newly independent nations went on to be governed by those trained by, and sympathetic to, the invaders. This resulted in the shameful neglect of the citizens of their own countries, whilst the land, it's resources, and people continued to service the former invader. Upon being ousted the invaders continued to exercise their might when they arbitrarily divided continents into countries, paying no heed to the more egalitarian land use of the original groups. This has been the major root cause of most of the warring amongst the peoples of Africa. And, though the history varies somewhat, it is the single, most significant cause for the frequent and the on going wars involving Israel since its installation on previously occupied lands.

Virtually every newly independent nation was left in destitution and devastation. The lands had become primarily single crop producers, the cultures had been devastated, men moved into urban areas by the droves to work the factories for export items, not making enough money to send home, turning to alcohol, drugs, crime and prostitution. The women remained on the land, trying to subsist on minimal farming, done on tiny plots not used for export crops, nurturing children, the elderly and the infirm. Young girls moved into urban prostitution to help support their families in the rural areas.

The ones who continued to benefit from this next wave of exploitation were, once again, the ordinary citizens of the Western world, which now included North America, Australia and Japan as well as the previous European nations. They now enjoyed an even wider variety of cheaper consumable goods. Goods such as pineapple, soy, electronics, gems, precious metals, garments, shoes, furnishings, exotic foods and drinks, petroleum products (plastics, disposables, synthetic fabrics for clothing and home furnishings, cosmetics) and so much more.

Over the next half a century Western nations executed their neo-colonial agenda of taking from the poor to supply the rich by way of multinational corporations. Which, in effect, now do the job that was done centuries ago by the early explorers, missionaries and settlers of the colonial era. They exploit, abuse, and break the spirit of the peoples of the formerly occupied nations, solely to provide cheap (in cost and quality) goods for the monstrous appetite for material goods of Westernized peoples. More than that, they now exploit the peoples of any nation if a profit can be made, such as former members of the Soviet Union. Large sums of the profits are then used to buy influence in governments and to arrange international agreements favouring the corporations. In fact they are favored over sovereign nations, over human and civil rights, and possess more rights than the average citizen of any nation.

The former colonies were left with little, and most of what little they had was for export to allow the former masters to continue their internal vying for economic and political power. In order to secure a steady supply of resources the Western nations created various financial institutions to offer aid to the now underprivileged, culminating in what today are known as The World Bank and The International Monetary Fund. Both funded indirectly by taxpayers of wealthier nations. However, aid was, and still is, not given without severe conditions, called Structural Adjustments to local affairs, in order to guarantee the repayment of the loans. These conditions have included privatization of local water, medical care, and transportation; use of expensive Western expertise and contractors for local projects; imposition of projects such as the building of unneeded infrastructures like dams that were never completed; of levies and taxes on essential survival goods; fees for services such as schooling and health care; purchase of Western made goods; monopolies for Western media, entertainment and advertisers.

To nations left with little, the few resources available have had to be used to service the interest on the loans, leaving the populace even more poverty stricken under the extreme demands of structural adjustments. For decades the former colonies have been sending much, much more in interest payments and in kind, to the Western nations than they have received in aid. The wealthy nations continue to get wealthier at the expense of those who can least afford it.

Of the many consequences the following are amongst the most significant. Along with The World Bank and The I.M.F., the World Trade Organization and international trade agreements have created the conditions that have impoverished even further peoples who were already near destitution when they gained their independence from centuries of brutal occupation. These organizations and agreements have made it virtually impossible for nations to establish their own laws, regulations and standards should these interfere with profits. Hence, there are few, if any, labour laws, environmental standards, or human rights regulations. The former colonies, or The Majority World, have become home to sweat shops, employing more than three hundred million children alone in dirty, dangerous, and hazardous conditions, turning out cheap consumer goods, and simultaneously generating profits in the billions for millionaire corporations. It is a very well documented myth that these children make enough money to support their families. They do not. Furthermore, they are abused and subjected to workplace and environmental dangers. If the pay really is sufficient then why not employ the parents and allow the children a safe, happy childhood? Is it because children are more gullible, easier to manipulate, and it is harder to abuse an adult, without the world coming to know of it?

Another consequence of the existence of multinational monopolies is the culture portrayed by the western mass media is being emulated worldwide, leading to the disintegration and loss of valuable ancient wisdom, and cultural diversity. Loss of either of these is dangerous for the survival of our species. Limiting our pool of knowledge also limits our options for survival. Further consequences are that public schools, health care, clean water, nutritious fresh food, life-fulfilling opportunities, and even dignity after death have become inaccessible to far too many in The Majority World. The position of women and girls has become even more precarious. The Majority World urban centers and rural life alike are both creating unprecedented levels of land, sea and air pollution, though minor compared with The Minority World.

One of the most heartbreaking consequences is that some of the formerly colonized, and now westernized, take it upon themselves to trash everything about their former culture. For instance there are Indians who trash Ayurvedic living, Chinese who trash Traditional Chinese Medicine, Africans who trash the Songoma, and African Americans who trash the genuine spirituality of Voodoo. The ultra-westernized now find loathing in everything about their pre-colonial culture, and this is reinforced daily through school curricula, university texts, and the giant conglomerates of global mass media of the Western Minded.

The invaders also took it upon themselves to drawn new political lines on maps when they divided colonies after the E.W. 2., following resource based criteria, not traditional use. With no regard to how the pre-existing nations had managed their boundaries, the new divisions gave rise to much of the current civil unrest worldwide. Now many people of the Majority World are living in poverty, unable to care for their families, unable to live by their own beliefs, unable to be heard, unable to defend themselves against the onslaught of cultural colonization, and unable to enjoy the fruits of their traditional lands and lives. The Indigenous of Latin America, the Arabs, the tribes of Africa, the peasants of India, the women around the world, and other groups are all rising up to free them-selves to live a life of dignity and meaning, as they see fit; not as the Western Minded wealthy elite see fit. Some turn to armed conflict, others to protests, others to legal venues, others appeal to the international community, and some simply disappear. Too many pay the price of lost lives, lost limbs, lost livelihoods, lost cultures, lost wisdoms, whilst a minority continues to reap the benefits.

The most insidious consequence of all is that some of the aid agreements entail the purchase of arms from donor countries in exchange for the few export items that the aid recipient nations produce. This continues to deprive an already deprived people of essentials and contributes to the militarization of the planet, consuming one trillion dollars annually. One one-hundredth of that budget would eradicate most of the crises facing humanity today; environmental pollution, climate change, species and cultural extinction, nuclear waste, lack of universal health care, education, clean water, poverty, desertification, homelessness and more could be eradicated with in one single generation.

Almost simultaneously to the above events of the past 50–60 years in the West, many of the social justice movements began to have an impact, as did new spiritual movements, while organized religions began to see a decline in membership. Women and minorities began to influence policy and social norms. International communication and transportation systems became accessible to most, and transnational organizations, such as The Red Cross and U.N.I.C.E.F., began to play significant roles globally. On the negative side, fundamentalism among all faiths started to rise, as did the need for Western capitalism to create an enemy after the fall of the Communist Soviet Union. So too rose the power of the profits of multinational corporations, and the destruction of the largest living organism in our solar system, the life-sustaining biosphere of planet Earth, named "Gaia" by Dr. James Lovelock.

Which finally brings us to today and to the Western Mind, a characteristic of most of the population of the Minority World. Those who qualify for membership are no longer members by virtue of location within a Western nation. They are found in every part of the world, in almost every religion, in every colour of skin, and are much like spoiled, self-absorbed adolescents. They are the ones who have allowed their minds to be colonized and become the beneficiaries of all that the neo-colonial agenda provides; designer labels, addictions to name brands, apathy towards the underdog, spiritual bankruptcy, and continuous self-gratification. In short they indulge in excessive consumption of material goods, dispose of everything, and frequently display a deficit of awareness of their connectedness to global issues. Often they will mock those who would endanger their comforts by the examples of their lives. Taking a stand on an issue of substance would be as foreign to them as cooking a meal at home of natural whole foods. However, they could discuss fashion ad nauseam. The worldwide dispersal of the Western Mind is a direct consequence of physical colonization first, and then mental colonization perpetrated by the corporations of the West that control the media, advertising agencies, the entertainment industry, and governments. Incidentally, the general, global lack of respect for Western morality is also a result of the monopolies held by the entertainment industries of the West, which inflict Western porn into the mud huts in rural planet Earth.

We, of the Diaspora of the Western Minded nation, are the direct beneficiaries of centuries of wrongs that continue into today. Individually we did not colonize anyone, we did not enslave anyone, we did not rape and pillage lands and people, we did not commit genocide, nor did we perpetuate any one of the other thousand wrongs. But, we do benefit from every one of the wrongs that was and is being committed for our comfort and convenience today.

If one could consider a spectrum on Western Mindedness, most of us in The Minority World would be somewhere on it. Gandhi ji and Mother Theresa would be fairly low on the spectrum. At the very top would be right winged, fundamentalist, neo-conservatives, such as Steven Harper, George Bush, Tony Blair, John Howard, Pope Benedict, and the C.E.O.s of most multinational corporations. There are few on this planet who would not qualify for a spot on the spectrum. Some of us have moved down a little, and some a lot as our awareness has grown, others have remained static and the largest number have moved up the scale. The challenge for all of us is to locate ourselves on the spectrum, in earnest, and then begin the journey downward at whatever pace is manageable. At every step ask yourself the question Gandhi ji would have asked of himself: how does this action help the least amongst us?

We, of the Western Mind are frequently lazy, thoughtless, uneducated, though often well schooled, malnourished of spirit, insecure, and addicted to convenience, instant gratification, appearance, and charity. The latter comforts us and keeps us from addressing the reason why conditions exist that create a need for charity. We are like The Borg, in assimilating cultures or destroying them if they resist, as we pursue our insatiable quest for consumables, at an ever-increasing pace, and at an ever-decreasing price. We comprise about 20 % of the world's population, use over 80% of its resources, and individually have an ecological footprint that is nearly one hundred times that of an individual from the Majority World. We are very much like indulged adolescents, and it is time to grow up.

The major world problems have little to do with birth control in the Majority World; they have everything to do with birth control in the Minority World. A child raised by Western Minded parents has an ecological footprint equivalent to one hundred children raised by the poor. Perhaps it would be much wiser for the Western Minded to stop reproducing themselves if they are really serious about world peace and harmony.

The path being recommended is not for the faint of heart. However, it will strengthen your heart and aid your evolution as you become a better parent, a better neighbor, a better global citizen, and a more profoundly compassionate human being that any child would be proud to call their hero.

Every journey begins with a single step. Your first one has been to read thus far, and the next one is to remain to read the rest. Congratulations! In the next several chapters the reader will be offered some insights, some solutions and then given several personal, local and global benefits of pursuing the advice. Once the global links have been established with a given solution offered the links might not be repeated in subsequent solutions. The intent is to initially help the reader connect the dots. After a few examples the reader will no doubt be able to connect the dots themselves.

If each Western Minded person were to change one thing only every month for one year, there would be nearly 18 billion positive changes for all of Life (20% of the global population times 12 months). Imagine what we could make happen if we continued with the positive changes at an even more accelerated pace for the remainder of each of our lifetimes! And, imagine what our children will have learned by our example! Imagine what a paradise we could leave future generations!

"The strongest impetus for creating a peaceful world is the genuine understanding of the ultimate value of Life, which transcends differences in nationality, race, gender, creed and species."
           H. P. Kaur, Global Education: A Movement And Methodology, 1993

CHAPTER SIX:

THE MAJOR ISSUES

Unto my bosom why do you point
Your bare bayonets?
This is your own abode
My friend, this heart of mine.
I fear your blows
Might not hurt yourself;
Our lives are intertwined
As they are.
                    Gurmukh Singh Musafir

If one considers oneself to be at the center point of a circle with the circle forming one's physical, bodily, occupied universe, then there exist ever enlarging concentric circles of issues, starting with the self and building out towards the entire Cosmos, some running through all the circles. Hunger can be just a personal issue and it certainly is a global issues. Air pollution can be just a personal issue for those with respiratory problems, but it is also an issue for every woman, man and child, everywhere. The focus of this work is mostly on global issues; that is, it is about those issues that effect a majority of Life on Earth.

The following list of such issues is a work in progress, which the author hopes will reduce to a blank page within her lifetime. However, that will be entirely up to the readers and to those who become the messengers once they receive the message.

MAJOR GLOBAL ISSUES CAUSING GLOBAL PROBLEMS

1   Children are not being raised to feel secure emotionally, physically, intellectually, or spiritually, and grow up into the adults who create all the following problems.

2   The practices of homophobia and misogyny have now become endemic to all parts to the world, and it is the hatred of feminine values that has produced so many of the global injustice issues. (Note that there is no equivalent word for the fear and hatred of maleness as there is for femaleness in the word "misogyny".).

3   Schooling has been confused with education, producing many successive generations of dysfunctional people, holding the limited worldview inherent in the current model of schooling, and creating a cheap labour force for large corporations.

4   The World Trade Organization, The International Monetary Fund, The World Bank, and parts of the United Nations being synonyms for the U.S.A., and its agenda for a USonian planetary empire.

5   The rise of: the neo-conservative, right-winged, fundamentalist agenda, religious indoctrination, and religion based charities.

6   Increased numbers of persons being persecuted, tortured, abused, disappeared, and increased number of human rights violations of people of conscience, and/or of different worldviews,

7   The unchecked power of international financial institutions, structural adjustment programs, and Majority World debt.

8   The effects of global warming, climate change, environmental pollutants leading to: rising rates of cancers, increased species extinction, desertification, deforestation, siltation, soil depletion, dangers of the Sun's rays, natural resource depletion, human created natural disasters, and environmental and political refugees.

9   Multi national, giant, conglomerates of corporations having more rights than humans and sovereign states, holding monopolies of the basics for survival, having patents and powers enshrined in laws for decades, having too much influence and control over governments, and having monopolies over the global mainstream mass media (The Trash Media).

10   Biotechnology, genetically modified foods, and the commodification of living things, and the ensuing problems.

11   Cultural extinction, theft of intellectual property rights, monoculture-ism.

12 Rogue nation domination, exploitation, illegal foreign invasion, belligerence, terrorism; production, sale and amassment
of weapons of mass destruction; testing of nuclear weapons,
and use of chemical and biological warfare.

13 Threat of nuclear war, warfare and related violence, weapon-
ization of space.

14 Poverty, hunger, homelessness,

15 Global epidemics, diseases, illness, and the heartlessness of
the multi-billion dollar pharmaceutical industry.

16 Lack of universal health for most of humanity, and health
issues including cancer, A.I.D.S., and malaria. (Half of all
North Americans will get cancer, nearly 90% of cancers are
environment related, and cancer is the second biggest killer
of our children.)

17 Overpopulation of the Western Minded, who are the largest
contributors to the overuse of fossil fuels and hydroelectric
power, leading to global warming, climate change, ill health,
illegal occupations and warfare.

18 Indentured labour of over three hundred million minors in
sweatshops, and other dangerous and hazardous jobs to supply
cheap goods for the materially addicted Western Minded.

19 Global drug trafficking, crime, prostitution, slave trade and
racketeering.

20 Enforced mal-development of the Majority World, through
the policies of the Western Minded Minority World.

21 The heroes of our children are not their parents, but movie
stars, music stars, athletes, and the very wealthy.

22 Missionaries!

Why missionaries?

For as far back as we have records, we seem to have some evidence of missionaries of sorts, generally well meaning, nearly always misguided. Just as it is always the insecure person who finds it necessary to convert others to their way of thinking, so too is it with religious missionaries as a group. They may actually believe they are doing the work of their god, and feel a need to convert everyone to their worldview. And, one must admit, it is hard to resist an all expense paid, extended vacation to some of the most beautiful locations on this planet. To date, too many missionaries have committed too many ungodly wrongs on the innocent for centuries, in every corner of the world, in the name of their god. It was with the colonial missionaries that the cycle of abuse and addiction began for First Peoples and other traditional cultures. It was the belief of the missionaries in their right to have dominion over all of creation that has created a planet filled with dysfunctional, converted people abusing their dominion. Since then other insidious groups have joined in the circle of abusers; corporations, despots, and the Western Minded neo-colonialist.

Having traveled, and borne witness to the damage done by many current missionaries I am loathe to see any more of them go off anywhere. The spiritual landscape at home is pretty bleak, and the missionaries need to clean up their own culture's religious and spiritual bleakness first. The problems elsewhere are perpetuated by the lifestyles, beliefs and attitudes of the flock at home. Please stay home and fix your own flock, so that the rest of the world does not continue to suffer from your flock's lack of a global conscience, and lack of an internal moral compass. You go to fix problems that can only be fixed by your own flock in your own back yards. The millions of dollars wasted on supporting missionaries worldwide, mostly donated and/or raised by the women, would build hospitals, schools, homes and more where these are desperately needed. So please, if you truly wish to do your lord's work, then just send money and stay home to clean your own house. Thanks, but no thanks!

SOME SIMPLE SOLUTIONS

No doubt some readers will be in disbelief that, for example, nursing babies can work towards halting nuclear weapon amassment, global warming, and species extinction. However, the author urges the readers to keep reading; the lines that connect the dots between personal actions and global issues will soon begin to form a big picture. Thereafter, all that will be needed will be for the reader to take to heart the information presented and begin to implement the solutions. Not all the following solutions will be explored in detail, however all will be implied in the solutions presented. The reader ought to become adept at understanding these implications upon completion of this work.

The solutions may appear too simplistic to be effective. They were not pulled out of a magic hat; they are based on a lifetime of study, work, and experience. A lifetime that has spanned more than half a century, and has gone from an outhouse and a daily milking of the family cow in India, to a life of comfort and plenty in Yuppyville. A lifetime that has known how it feels to use a women's shelter, how it feels to use a food bank to feed three babies, and how it feels to be on the brink of bankruptcy for endless years as a single parent of three. A lifetime passionately devoted to a love of higher learning, of needing to understand, and of wanting to share the messages learned. A lifetime that has seen the effects of even the smallest acts to make a big difference, in particular in the acts in making children feel secure.

It is not the intent of the author to list every possible issue and solution, nor discuss each implication of every possible scenario. That would be far too monumental and certainly beyond the scope of this work and the expertise of this author. The intent is to whet the appetite enough to inspire the readers to find their own creative solutions to all that ails humanity. As the work of only one mind, it is improbable just one author could pose and/or answer all possible questions. The readers are strongly encouraged to seek their own answers to the hard questions, and to be fearless in asking them of all the sources that need to be questioned.

OF UTMOST URGENCY IN RESOLVING ALL MAJOR GLOBAL ISSUES:

RAISE CHILDREN IN WAYS THAT WILL MAKE THEM FEEL SECURE EMOTIONALLY, PHYSICALLY, INTELLECTUALLY AND SPIRITUALLY.

AND THE COROLLARY TO THAT BEING:

RAISE THE STATUS OF PARENTING TO WELL ABOVE THAT OF EVERY OTHER VOCATION, BE IT THAT OF PRIME MINISTER, POPE, PRINCE, OR PRINCIPLE SHARE HOLDER.

What follows are suggestions that are guaranteed to lead us in the right direction to achieving a fair and safe world for all. The first twenty are discussed in detail and the dots are connected for the reader. For the remainder, the reader is urged to find the links and connect the dots for themselves.

1   Nurse babies, and make baby food at home.

2   Work outside the home less and prepare whole foods for your children, preferably organic, and <u>never</u> frequent McGarbage type fast food outlets.

3   Use natural materials in caring for your children and family.

4   Provide children with limited amounts of "stuff", made of natural material.

5   Learn about and teach children what is currently known about the nature of reality.

6   Teach our boys "girl" things.

7   Keep corporations out of our schools, colleges and universities.

8   Stop fundraising for schools by selling processed foods and drinks, petroleum based trinkets, and other non-essential items.

9   Model, teach, reinforce, and reward use of the twelve universal values of the Living Values Education Program.

10 Lobby your school board to provide staff with in-service training in media literacy, and ensure that students, parents and the community receive it also.

11 Avail yourself of your local library much more often than the local big box video store.

12 Lobby your school to employ teachers who are well trained global educators, in theory, practice and example.

13 Get rid of most of the channels on cable T.V., look to alternative media for more authentic information, and look to public T.V. more often for entertainment, education and information.

14 Establish a regular spiritual practice (It seems we are hard-wired for spiritual maturity.)

15 Eliminate use of all disposables.

16 Eat much less animal protein.

17 Buy local, union made goods, and do not support the foreign owned big box store chains.

18 Use only biodegradable, cruelty free, minimally packaged cleansers, yard, garden and car care products.

19 Use only biodegradable, cruelty free toiletries and cosmetics.

20 Retrofit your home for energy efficiency, and keep vehicles well tuned.

21 Women, become media literate!

22 Men, learn about ecological feminism and liberation theology.

23 Remove all gender specific toys, and all war toys from your home, replacing them with your ACTIVE will to nurture children's wellbeing.

24 Overcome your schooling and get educated.

25 Invest in ethical funds only.

26 Get up early enough to make a nourishing breakfast, and wholesome lunches (placed in permanent use containers and bags), for your family, and cook a healthy dinner together.

27 Stop recycling! **REDUCE! REDUCE! REDUCE CONSUMPTION!** Recycling is asinine for the most part, only giving permission to the wealthy to continue over consumption. Reuse everything possible, and as a very last step recycle what can no longer be used as is (to recycle means to convert the materials in the item into something else useful – trading clothing is not recycling, that is reusing).

28 Learn about major world faiths and practice your own in greater earnest.

29 Believe nothing and believe no one source, find out for yourself.

30 Practice good health and wellbeing through natural means, and take a holistic (allopathic and naturopathic together) approach to health care.

31 Tune out all advertising of non-survival products.

32 Develop natural good looks from the inside with your diet and lifestyle, not with externally applied products, ingested chemicals and medical procedures.

33 Do some daily physical activity; a family walk serves many good ends.

34 Stop competing with the Joneses (they've probably got cancer, heart disease, addictions, apathy, hardening of the attitudes and spiritual vacancy) and instead compete with who you were yesterday.

35 Overcome your addiction to convenience.

36 Use natural materials in buildings, furnishings, décor and accessories.

37 Denounce the God of Consumer Goods and his Advertising Apostles, and exercise your purchasing power to exorcise them both.

38 Don't make more efficient what ought not to have been done in the first place (E.g.; processing and bottling water, given that 75% of the planet was unpolluted water when the human race arrived of late).

39 Every time you want to buy "stuff", ask your self two things: why am I really buying it, and how much harm has already happened to Others in producing this thing?

40 Learn to live by THE THREE RS OF BEING HUMAN: RESPECT, RESTORE, AND REVERE ALL OF LIFE.

Because,

"IT IS BETTER TO LIGHT A CANDLE THAN TO CURSE THE DARK,"

Ralph Waldo Emerson

SOME NOT SO SIMPLE SOLUTIONS

The following are just a few suggestions for those who wish to go to the next step. It is of little value to do most of these without first addressing the above listed work of changing one's own actions which cause the problems. It would be a little like a child molester lobbying for tougher sentencing for child molesters. All the solutions recommended would further the goals of peace, justice and security for all of Life. The links may be unclear at this point; however, once the links are made for the solutions in subsequent pages the reader should be able to return to the following and extrapolate the links for themselves.

1 Create a society in which parenting has the highest status of all jobs.

2 Raise secure children.

3 Lobby for much greater incentives for farmers to farm organically, and elevate the status of farming to just below that of parenting.

4 Lobby for a universal health care system that makes greater provisions for proactive holistic, naturopathic living than our current allopathic drug induced reactive living does.

5   Become involved in existing social justice movements.

6   Write letters to elected leaders, newspapers and to appropriate web sites on matters of social justice for all.

7   Learn how you are governed, get involved, and vote for candidates with the best record of community service and integrity, regardless of political affiliation.

8   Learn why affirmative action exists and support it.

9   Question current assumptions, be they social, academic, philosophical, political, or religious.

10 Develop your inner landscape, not your material landscape.

11 Learn how to address the issues that initially lead to social injustice.

12 Volunteer at food banks and shelters AND work on the root causes that give rise to both of these.

13 Keep missionaries at home where they will do less damage, and clean your own back yard first.

14 Donate to good causes and accept nothing in exchange: no galas, no bracelets, no tokens, no tax breaks, no nothing! If you can afford to donate you do not need any perks, and the money wasted on your unnecessary perks is desperately needed elsewhere.

15 Lobby for change in government, corporations, and international financial institutions to ensure the basic needs of all are met.

16 Take eco-friendly and culturally sensitive vacations.

17   Facilitate the resolution of wrongs done during and since colonization and now during neo-colonization.

18   Do not buy goods or services from any rogue nation, or visit the nation, or beam in its cultural colonization (written, audio, visual, or electronic), inform its governing body of the reasons for your actions and what it will take to win you back.

19   Stop corporate sponsorship in schools and universities, unless it comes with no strings and is advertising free.

20   Lobby your municipal government to charge a larger sum for every garbage bin of non-recyclables and plastics for curbside pick up, and offer a reward for every bag of recyclable glass, paper, aluminum, cardboard, newspapers and organic matter.

21   Turn your lawn into a haven of indigenous plants for local birds, bees and butterflies, and save on work, water, chemicals and money.

22   Do not patronize foreign owned big box stores (The Big B.S.), or foreign owned food and drink chains, or foreign owned entertainment facilities if they are doing any harm to anyone, in any way.

23   Let the Big B.S. human rights violators know that your favour will be regained if they demand, and only deal with, suppliers who pay fair wages, adhere to labor standards, create environmental protection, and hire adults instead of children.

24   Let the same Big B.S. know they too need to pay fair wages, benefits, and offer job security if you are to patronize them again.

25   Jealously guard and promote your national sovereignty.

26   Become an active part of the village that it takes to raise a child.

27   Once you get the message, become the messenger.

28   Befriend your local aboriginal community and learn their truth about the history and current situation of the land claims of the Indigenous of your country, and work for a fair and just settlement. You are, after all, a direct beneficiary of all the previously committed wrongs.

29   Lobby for more public transportation.

30   Have schools examine all curricula and resources for cultural biases, in service teachers to use these as teaching tools, and create more culturally appropriate and inclusive resources.

31   Model good manners, thoughtfulness, and courtesy.

32   Learn about the human conditions that give rise to crime, prostitution, drugs and other anti-social behavior, and work towards eliminating those conditions.

33   STOP BEING LAZY!!!!

34   Learn about the agenda of the current administration of the U.S.A., the W.T.O., World Bank, I.M.F., and some parts of the U.N., and then decide if they are essentially all different sides of the same trick coin.

35   Learn to govern and police yourself, simply because it is the right thing to do, and not for some reward or punishment from some external authority.

36   With every decision ask yourself, as Gandhi advised, how the decision may affect the least amongst us, and mostly ask if it is good for the children of the world.

SOME GOOD NEWS

1   There are many sources available from which/who to learn how to parent for a world filled with secure children.

2   There is easy access to global communication systems, supplying multiple viewpoints on current events and issues, almost instantly.

3   Transnational agencies, such as The Red Cross, are able to report a bigger truth than the Trash Media does presently.

4   The rising interest in The Slow Food movement, now slowly transforming into The Slow Living Movement.

5   Greater cross-cultural communication allowing for greater understanding ("If necessity was the mother of invention, then information is the mother of understanding," Dr. Donovan Jones, my philosophy of religion professor).

6   The establishment of The World Court, which is now able to prosecute individuals for crimes against humanity, except those committed by one belligerent rogue state.

7   A movement toward enlightened, substantive information about awareness of global issues.

8   The rise of spirituality, assisting humanity to first understand its connection to everything, and then how to act accordingly.

9   Cuba and Castro, as a model of how a tiny, poor country could be virtually self sufficient, have one of the highest rates of literacy, have universal health care and every other social service net, and be a constant thorn in the side of unbalanced capitalism.

10   Greater recognition of minority rights, at least in legislation

for a start.

11 Rising interest in holistic lifestyles.

12 The spreading of The Global Education movement and methodology into public schools and other institutions.

13 More children taking stands on issues of importance to them and to the world's children.

14 More men taking an interest in child rearing and caregiver roles.

15 Social justice movements having great success in keeping greedy corporations out of the pockets, natural resources, governance and lives of the people of The Majority World.

16 More and more people in The Minority World waking up to their complicity in global injustices.

17 The Living Values Education Program being taught in over eighty-four countries in more than thirty-five languages, in schools, refugee camps, and other settings.

18 The growth in numbers and power of civil society movements such as the World Social Forum.

19 The slowing down of the corporate agenda of the W.T.O, I.M.F, World Bank, and the G-8 through protests and information dissemination.

20 The ranking of nations by their H.D.I. (Human Development Index) instead of their G.D.P (Goddess D_____d Profits).

21 Slow and partial recognitions by the Catholic Church, some Protestant denominations, and some governments for wrongs committed while they were furthering their own selfish ends.

22   More opportunities for female education, beyond mere schooling.

23   The rise of interest in ecotourism.

24   The growth of the liberation theology and ecological feminism movements.

25   The longevity of Gene Roddenberry's vision, sans minor flaws.

26   The successes of the Council for a Parliament of World Religions, the International Association for Religious Freedom, and the International Association of Liberal Religious Women.

27   The World Indigenous Peoples Conferences on Education every three years.

28   The outrageously courageous Raging Grannies.

29   Conversion to mysticism by advanced quantum physicists.

30   Restorative justice finding its way into the current injustice system, which is only accessible to those with money.

31   The Sun continues to shine, the Earth continues to rotate, the tide continues to come and go, the wind continues to blow, and Life continues to celebrate itself with cyclic renewal.

CHAPTER SEVEN:

IN THE BEGINING

Your children are not your children.
They are the sons and daughters of Life's longing for itself.
They come through you but not from you.
And though they are with you yet they belong not to you.
You may give them your love but not your thoughts,
For they have their own thoughts.
You may house their bodies but not their souls,
For their souls dwell in the house of tomorrow, which you can not visit, not
      Even in your dreams.
You may strive to be like them, but seek not to make them like you.
For life goes not backwards, nor tarries with yesterday.
You are the bows from which your children as living arrows are sent forth.
The archer sees the mark upon the path of the infinite, and It bends you
      with Its might that Its arrow may go swift and far.
Let your bending in the archer's hand be for gladness,
For even as the archer loves the arrow that flies,
So the archer loves also the bow that is stable.
                    Kahlil Gibran

It has been said that children are our greatest resource. On the contrary, it is the adults who should be the greatest resource for the children. But it is not so for the Western Minded. From the evidence it is difficult to believe the Western Minded actually love their children, or care about their future wellbeing. It would be heartwarming to be proven wrong. Too frequently the Western Minded sacrifice their children for their own convenience, and for the sake of appearance. It almost appears as though they spend more time daily selecting their specialty coffee in some foreign owned coffee shop than they do speaking to their children about things that matter to the children.

By legal definition one is a child/youth until roughly 18-21 in most Minority World countries. Ironically, we allow the "child" to have legal sex and drive a lethal weapon at younger ages than we allow the "child" to vote as an adult. In ancient and older cultures a "child" became an adult with the performing of a coming of age ritual around the time of the onset of puberty. In either case, the passing from childhood into adulthood means the person is now to be considered a productive, independent member of the group. In either case it is a long, long time of dependency. No other species known to us has such a long, long period of childhood. And no other species seems to be as irresponsible in teaching essential survival skills, in spite of having more than a decade with each offspring, to do so.

The following are only a few examples of observations made over thirty-five years of teaching, in several countries, that support the assertion that Western Minded adults fail to be the greatest resource for their children, and in fact are the most neglectful of their children amongst all the known species. The neglect is serious enough to be considered abuse.

The term "Parents" is used to refer to whomsoever are the primary care givers. Of course, none of the readers of this work would be considered the parents described below. On the other hand, if the shoe fits ....

1. Western Minded parents pay more than triple per hour to their auto mechanic than to their childcare provider.

2. Western Minded parents repeatedly fill the children's lunch bags with prepackaged goods (bads?) that have NO nutritional value whatsoever, just for the convenience of it.

3. Western Minded parents supply the children with overpriced, unnecessary clothing, shoes, accessories, gadgets and "stuff", and then work long hours away from the children to pay for all the "stuff".

4. The children of Western Minded parents seem to lack good manners, fail to display common courtesy, and consistently show a sense of entitlement and selfishness.

5. Few, if any, of the Western Minded parents, nor teachers, nor other community leaders seem to be setting an example for consuming less, or for eating properly, or for staying fit in all aspects of human being, or showing a love of learning,

6. The children of Western Minded parents show boredom quickly at home without schoolwork for they do little to carry their own weight at home, and nor do they learn about responsibility to a group,

7. The heroes of the children of the Western Minded parent frequently are rock stars, athletes, movie stars, and the wealthy, who are famous, but have done little to make the world a better place.

8. Western Minded mothers are not nursing babies, too often because it is felt to be inconvenient or repugnant, and Western Minded parents are feeding heavily processed foods and drinks daily to their children.

9. The children of Western Minded parents are given televisions, computers, video games and other electronic childcare devices to keep them in their rooms, totally disengaged from human contact and unsupervised for hours on end.

10. The children of Western Minded parents seem to know little or nothing about being self sufficient adults able to cook, clean, launder, sew, budget, or do any one of the many tasks necessary to be an effective, productive, self suficient adult.

11. Western Minded parents spend hundreds of dollars a month on name brand clothes, electronic gadgets and disposable paper/plastic items, but balk at paying a few extra cents for organic food.

12. Western Minded parents allow their children to operate a lethal weapon at age sixteen and rarely talk about the significance of "sex, drugs and rock and roll" with their children.

13. Western Minded parents are quick to blame the school system for their child's lack of any success in schools, failing to examine their own role in how their child has been turning out.

14. Many Western Minded parents pay vast amounts for prestigious private schooling of the academic part of their children's intellect, and neglect to feed their children's bodies, minds, emotions, and intellect with all that is wholesome and good for balanced growth.

15. In Western Minded families very little, or no, attention is paid to the overt spiritual or emotional development of children. Parents seem to focus on a very limited development of the intellect and the physical; and even those are limited to academics and athletics, respectively. "If only a man's arms grew after birth, he would be considered a freakish monster," Mr. Desrocher, my Grade 12 French teacher.

16. Western Minded parents support the million dollar salaries for athletes by buying game tickets; brand name clothing and accessories, trinkets and sports memorabilia; and they then begrudge teachers, heath care and child care workers minor pay increases and improvements in working conditions for the benefit of the children.

17. Western Minded parents often frown upon their adolescent children working in the junk food industry on principle, and yet are proud of their children for learning to invest in oil companies.

18. Western Minded parents seem to treat their offspring as pawns in a game of whose child is smarter, faster, stronger, more accomplished, ….

19. Western Minded parents consistently set a bad example by giving in to the peer pressure of advertisers, modeling all the wrong things in expecting their children to not yield to peer pressure regarding "sex, drugs and rock and roll".

20. The average life expectancy of our children has become less than that of our generation's for the time in recorded history!!!!!!!!!!!!!!! This is all thanks to the lack of appropriate care from Western Minded parents.

These things, amongst others, all lead to vague feelings of insecurity in childhood, which naturally lead one to a lack of caring about others, whether they be next door or on the other side of the globe. Apathy fuels the ills of the world to grow. There are virtually no examples of secure adults who have turned to crime, drugs, prostitution, abuse of others, violence, or become burdens to society. It has always been the seriously insecure who have been the ones wreaking havoc on the innocent and upon themselves, be they dictators, elected presidents, schoolyard bullies, street walkers, the obscenely wealthy, child molesters, fundamentalists, control freaks, or alcoholics.

In thirty-five years of teaching, and many more as an adult, this author has never met a child who dreamed of growing up to be a drug addict. Or dreamed of growing up to be a prostitute, or a hardened criminal, or a despot, or any other form of a sociopath. No one aspires to become a sociopath; they are lead there by the actions and inactions of their caregivers and their community at large. This author has encountered many children who were already showing signs of becoming sociopaths, and one meeting with their parents often explained why.

In all the years of being alive, this author has never met a parent whose childhood dream was to become a bad parent. The cycle of bad parenting began somewhere, and must stop NOW if our species is to survive the self-destructive habits of the Western Minded. Raising secure children creates a society of secure adults, which in turn creates peace, harmony and contentment. Utopian thinking? Yes. Absolutely! We need look no further than many tribal societies to verify that raising secure children leads to greater happiness, contentment and peace for all. The study and pursuit of fulfilling every level of human need, as defined by Abraham Maslow, should be a requirement for all before they even consider conceiving a child. When one's lower level needs are appropriately and adequately met one is able to move up the levels with greater ease, aspiring to self-actualize, living a life of meaning.

Children are life's way of celebrating love, and need to be parented appropriately. It is not the primary responsibility of the television, or video games, or computers, or teachers to raise children. It is a parent's most important job. It is, in fact, the only job our species is required to do well in order to survive! It is, without a doubt, the most difficult job to do, and, perhaps, that is why so few of us lazy, Western Minded people choose to do it wholeheartedly, and why so many men have historically chosen to absent themselves from it all together.

There are many who will say, "Yeah but, my child will not do ……….,", or "Yeah but, my child does not like………..", or some other "Yeah buts!".

Who is the parent? Who is the responsible adult? Who is the grown up in this parent-child relationship?

Using the common vernacular, it could be said that parents are "copping out" of their responsibility by blaming their child, or even society, for not this, or not that, or wont this, or wont that. It could be that they themselves have had little or no modeling of good parenting, and need to learn that first for themselves. Or, maybe they are just too lazy. Parents, remember where the other three fingers point when pointing a finger of blame.

We make errors of commission, and equally seriously we make errors of omission. Both cause problems to develop. Each one of us is a part of the big picture of problems, and must become actively engaged in being a part of the solutions.

SOLUTION #1: NURSE BABIES, AND MAKE BABY FOOD AT HOME

BECAUSE IT WILL:

~ help the baby grow up feeling more secure in all aspects of being human
~ improve the child's health,
~ improve the mother-child relationship,
~ make universal health care a reality for all,
~ improve the environment,
~ reduce the incidence of cancer,
~ slow down climate change,
~ decrease environmental refugee numbers,
~ reduce the reasons for current wars,
~ reduce poverty in the Majority World,
~ **and SAVE MONEY.**

HOW IS THAT POSSIBLE?

A baby that is nursed receives necessary and easily digested nutrients, natural immunities and antibodies, and valuable physical and emotional contact. The mother is able to regain her pre-pregnancy body faster, and has greater bonding with the baby. The time required for nursing is time spent making the baby feel more secure. There is no waste involved, and no need of any external "stuff".

Other than the well known nutritional, health, and emotional benefits to both mother and child, nursing reduces the impact on the environment, as does feeding one's baby homemade baby food. Formula milk and baby food require natural ingredients; factories and manufacturing plants; artificial nutrients, flavors and colours; water; fossil fuel and hydroelectric energy;, transportation of ingredients, energy, packaging, manufacture equipment, and waste; advertising; manufacturing, transportation and disposal of waste packaging; and genetically modified crops, some grown by poor Majority World farmers for export in exchange for foreign debt relief.

Every item that is manufactured in factories creates pollutants for the air, land and water during the process, and then more in creating the packaging, then even more in the transporting of it, and finally in the disposing of the packaging. Canadians are amongst the top five nations for making garbage per person and amongst the last for reclaiming, reducing or recycling. All our garbage is burned, buried, or shipped to other nations, often the Majority World countries, in exchange for a pittance. Creating land, water and air pollution here and abroad.

Baby food and formula are manufactured in factories. Factories manufacturing any goods create environmental conditions that contribute to global warming and climate change. Climate change has already created environmental refugees in the poorest parts of the world, extreme weather planet wide, species extinction, infestations unknown before in given climatic regions, forest fires, floods, and property damage in the millions of dollars.

Cancer is the second largest killer of N. American children, and nearly 90% of all cancers are related to environmental pollutants. Diet and life style are also highly complicit in the poor health of our children, who now suffer from adult inflictions such as diabetes, heart disease, and obesity. Diet, lifestyle, and quality of the environment are all within our control. Are the children worth the inconvenience to the Western Minded adults?

Homemade baby food is far more nutritious, cheaper, better quality, and contains no toxins if made with organic, whole foods. Both nursing and homemade foods reduce illness, and therefore help to keep public health care costs down. This is generally not an issue for the Western Minded, but their abuse of the system through neglect of their own, and of their children's nutritional needs is an issue for the rest of us.

The resources needed for the packaging, transportation and manufacture are mostly petroleum products, and wars and occupations today are over the control of this resource. Furthermore, less than 5% of the environmental damage to oceans is the result of oil spills; it is the result of the shipping of petroleum on the oceans for processing into disposable packaging, and other plastic products, all for our excessive, unnecessary use of energy.

Prepared baby foods and formula often contain soy, corn, sugar, and dairy products. The corn and soy are genetically modified, grown with dangerous fertilizers, pesticides, fungicides, and herbicides. Dairy products are obtained from factory-farmed cows, loaded with antibiotics and unnatural growth hormones. Much of the feed for dairy cattle is exported from the Majority World, as is sugar, where both are produced without labor or environmental regulations. The land and crops that should be feeding the poorest are instead being used to make export items for creating toxins to feed children of the wealthiest.

There are circumstances that make it impossible to nurse a baby, they do not include laziness, appearance, or inconvenience. Nursing and making baby food are dramatically more cost effective than buying prepared formula or food, and both contribute towards global peace and security for all.

If the dots connected have shown the reader the global impact to peace, human rights, environment and equitable development, then the only reason for continuing the practices of baby formula and prepared foods would be laziness. Lack of knowledge is no excuse for the Western Minded, who most certainly do have easy access to abundant resources for information.

See chart #1 page 76
See chart #2 page 82

CHART #1: ON BABY FORMULAE AND PREPARED INFANT FOODS AND DRINKS

BABY FORMULAE AND PREPARED INFANT FOODS AND DRINKS REQUIRE THE FOLLOWING RESOURCE (bold print below), WHICH REQUIRE OTHERS (lettered a, b, c, ... , and then indicated by ◊), AND HAVE THE LISTED GLOBAL EFFECTS (last column with each item below).

TRANSPORT

a) **fossil fuels** ◊ extraction from the Earth——————————— ◊ Environmental damage to land, sea and air, promotes wars

◊ energy ——————————————————— ◊ Environmental damage to land, sea and air, promotes wars

◊ machinery ———————————————— ◊ Manufacture damages environment and depletes resources

b) **roads** ◊ construction machinery ——————————— ◊ Manufacture damages environment and depletes resources

◊ fossil fuels——————————————— ◊ Add to green house gasses, climate change, and global warming

◊ land——————————————————— ◊ Effects natural pathways, increased road kill

◊ vehicles ◊factories ———————————— ◊ Manufacture of these adds to environmental pollutants

◊ fossil fuels ————————————— ◊ Extraction and use increase global warming

◊ metal, plastic, wood, fabric, and glass - ◊ All created in factories, causing increased pollution

MANUFACTURE

a) **factories** ◊ building and equipment ———————————— ◊ Require materials made in factories, adding to pollution, depletion of green space and natural resource, species extinction, reduced capacity for air cleaning, increase in greenhouse gas effects, promote global warming and climate change.

b) **energy** ◊ fossil fuels——————————————— ◊ add to environmental pollution, promote wars over control of petroleum, oceans and marine life dying due to damage during shipping of petroleum, pristine areas being mined for coal in environmentally harmful ways, increase in greenhouse gasses, global warming, and climate change.

◊ Natural waterways are dammed to obtain it, flooding habitat, species extinction increased, unsuccessful relocation of already marginalized peoples, use of fossil fuels in production increases global warming and climate change

◊ hydroelectric fuel ----

◊ See below under "Other Ingredients"

c) ingredients   ◊ see below ----

RETAIL FACILITY

a) building   ◊ land----

◊ For every building there is a decrease in green space and clean air

b) equipment ----

◊ All are made in factories, increasing pollution, depleting resources

c) parking lot   ◊ land----

◊ Every building / parking lot decreases green space and clean air

d) energy for operations ◊ fossil fuels ----

◊ Extraction and use add to global warming, climate change, and warfare

◊ hydroelectric----

◊ Damming of waterways causes environmental damage, and relocation

CROPS

a) if organically farmed ◊ land----

◊ Soil nutrients are replenished

◊ water----

◊ No toxic contamination of ground water

◊ sun ----

◊ Nothing to negatively effect greenhouse gasses

◊ air ----

◊ No toxic off gassing

◊ natural fertilizers, pesticide, herbicides, fungicides ----

◊ Replenish essential nutrients, increase nutritional value of crop

◊ labour intensive, less farm machinery ----◊ manual labour does virtually no damage

b) if chemically farmed

◊ land ----◊ soil nutrients depleted

◊ water ----◊ communal ground water contaminated by chemical nutrients

◊ sun ----◊ manufacture, packaging, shipping, use of chemicals adds to green-house gasses and pollution

◊ air ----◊ off gassing, manufacture, packaging and shipping add to air pollution

◊ chemical fertilizers, pesticides, herbicides, fungicides ----◊ deplete soil nutrients and crop nutrition, add toxins to crops, land, and water

◊ farm machine intensive----◊ severe negative effects on land, water, air

OTHER INGREDIENTS

a) flavours, colours, preservatives

◊ chemicals ----◊ made in factories, adding to pollution, depletion of natural resources

◊ energy----◊ fossil and hydroelectric fuel, increasing global warming and pollution

◊ factories ----◊ see FACTORIES above

b) seasonings

◊ farming ----◊ see CROPS above

◊ factories ----◊ see FACTORIES above

c) sugars

◊ overseas plantations ----◊ deprive poor of food crops, no labour or environmental standards

◊ transportation from overseas ----◊ see TRANSPORTATION above

◊ processing facilities----◊ see FACTORY above

d) meat and dairy products

◊ factory farms ----◊ contamination of land, ground water, and aiir

◊ feed ◊ crops ----◊ see CROPS above

◊ drugs ◊ manufacture ◊ see MANUFACTURE, also these toxins accumulate in human bodies

◊ water----------- ◊ being contaminated faster than Earth is able to replenish fresh water

PACKAGING

a) factory ◊ land, energy, equipment ---------- ◊ see FACTORY above

b) transport ◊ see above for requirements---------- ◊ see TRANSPORT above

c) energy ◊ fossil and hydroelectric---------- ◊ see above

d) petroleum for plastic packaging---------- ◊ see Fossil Fuels above

e) wood for paper packaging ---------- ◊ reduces air quality, increases siltation, destroys habitat, increases greenhouse gasses and global warming

ADVERTISING

a) agency ◊ building ◊ see above---------- ◊ Reduces green space, air quality and natural resources

b) clever people ◊trained at taxpayers expense ---------- ◊ Wastes talent for ill gotten gains

c) appropriate resources ---------- ◊ Depleting natural resources

d) media ◊ print, audio, visual, electronic ---------- ◊ All requiring resources, and adding to brain washing

WASTE DISPOSAL

a) from manufacturing ◊created in manufacturing ---------- ◊ Depletion of natural resources, increase in pollution and global warming

◊ transport to disposal site ---------- ◊ Depletion of natural resources, increase in pollution and global warming

b) from retail outlet ◊ same as above ---------- ◊ Depletion of natural resources, increase in pollution and global warming

c) from consumer ◊ same as above ---------- ◊ Depletion of natural resources, increase in pollution and global warming

IN SUMMARY, THESE ARE THE NET RESULTS OF THE CONVENIENCE OF FEEDING BABIES FORMULA MILK AND GIVING INFANTS PROCESSED, PRE-PREPARED FOODS:

1   They contain little nutrition compared to nursing and home made organic, whole foods. And, pound for pound cost astronomically more. Even if the raw ingredients are organic, there is a great deal less nutrition in these than organic, home made, fresh ones.

2   Toxins from artificial flavours, colours, preservatives accumulate in baby and infant bodies. The damage done to the environment during all the manufacturing processes harms the baby's health, and the health of all living things.

3   The extent of the environmental damage done by the sum of all the processes involved includes the following:
    ~ increase in rates of cancer
    ~ increase in respiratory problems
    ~ increase in greenhouse gasses
    ~ increase in global warming
    ~ increase in rates of climate change
    ~ increase in extreme, unpredictable weather
    ~ decrease in natural resources
    ~ increase in ocean pollution due to shipping of petroleum
    ~ increase in rates of species extinction

4   Limited natural resources are being depleted, to create foods that are harmful to babies. More medical services are needed due to poor diet, and due to environment related illnesses, placing further strain on health care, giving impetus to governments to abandon universal health care in favour of private health care.

5   Current wars and occupations enable rogue states to control limited resources of our only Earth. These same rogue states continue to manufacture, distribute, and amass weapons of mass destruction in order to maintain control of limited resource. Thus, controlling the world. Wars are inevitably over the control of limited planetary resources, leading to further weapons amassment, including nuclear,

biological and chemical. Wasteful use of natural resources promotes wars.

6   Chemical farming processes that grow crops for baby food deplete soil nutrients and food nutrients, and they pollute the ground water, land and air. Industrial farming of livestock and dairy cattle do the same damage, and add to the greenhouse effect.

7   The disposal of the waste created through out all the processes further pollutes ground water, the soil and air, and negatively effects our Sun's rays. The farming, manufacturing, transporting, and waste disposal processes add to the conditions that increase global warming, and climate change,

8   Valuable land is wasted in converting good crops into toxic waste fed to westernized babies and infants, while millions in The Majority World go hungry. The use of Majority World lands for crops for export and for dumping ground for our waste creates further hardship for already impoverished people.

9   Some of the toxic chemicals digested by infants are ultimately flushed into the communal ground water system, for other innocents to digest.

TO CONTINUE TO FEED BABIES CONVENEINT FORMULA AND CONVENIENT PROCESSED FOODS IS A SILENT, VERY INCONVENIENT HOMICIDE OF ALL SPECIES. IT IS LABOUR INTENSIVE AND TIME CONSUMING TO NURSE BABIES AND TO FEED THEM ORGANIC, HOME MADE, WHOLE FOODS. IT IS HOMICIDE, SUICIDE AND CERTAIN INFANTICIDE TO CONTINUE TO FEED BABIES CHEMICAL FORMULAE AND CHEMICALLY GROWN PROCESSED FOODS SIMPLY BECAUSE IT IS CONVENIENT.

CHART #2; ON NURSING BABIES AND HOME MAKING WHOLE FOODS FOR INFANTS

NURSING BABIES AND MAKING ORGANIC, WHOLE FOODS FOR INFANTS REQUIRE CERTAIN RESOURCES AND HAVE THE FOLLOWING LISTED EFFECTS;

NURSING

a) time

b) lactating female

c) adequate nourishment

}

1 There are virtually no adverse side effects to the environment or to any species, in particular if the female/mother consumes organic, whole foods and drinks.

2 There are many physical, and psychological health and rest for mother benefits, and there is no waste requiring disposal.

HOME MADE, ORGANIC, WHOLE FOODS AND DRINKS FOR INFANTS

SEE CHART #3 (page 88) for the effects and consequences of consuming pre-prepared, pre-packaged, processed foods and drinks.

SEE CHART #4 (page 93) for the effects and consequences of consuming home made organic, whole foods and drinks.

THE HEALTH AND WELLBEING BENEFITS CONFIRED UPON ALL OF LIFE THROUGH THESE TWO SIMPLE ACTS ARE TOO NUMEROUS TO NOT PERSUE VIGOROUSLY IF ONE IS TRULY SERIOUS ABOUT A WORLD OF PEACE AND SECURITY FOR ALL OF LIFE.

82

SOLUTION #2: WORK OUTSIDE THE HOME LESS AND PREPARE ORGANIC, WHOLE FOODS FOR CHILDREN

BECAUSE IT WILL:

~ make the children more secure and
~ smarter in school,
~ improve your family's health and wellbeing,
~ lower health care costs,
~ make universal health care more accessible to all,
~ reduce environmental toxins,
~ lower rates of global warming,
~ reduce the amount of waste needing management,
~ replenish the severely depleted farm soils,
~ curb the genetic modification frenzy of food,
~ reduce our petroleum addiction,
~ reduce armed conflict and W.M.D. amassment,
~ **and SAVE MONEY.**

HOW IS THAT POSSIBLE?

It is said that money can not buy love, and yet nearly 75 % of families, with pre-school age children, in N. America employ a substitute parent to fulfill the caregiver role, because both parents have gone outside the home to earn money. Most of the hired parents are themselves mothers, whose own children suffer from lack of real parenting as much as the children of the wealthier Western Minded suffer. The U.N. Declaration of the Rights of the Child specifically enshrines a child right to be with her/his own parents, and neither the Western Minded nor the underpaid substitute parent are able to comply with that. Having raised three children alone I understand the need for many single parents to employ a substitute parent. I also know that by doing many of the things I recommend I needed a lot less money, and thus I was able to work part time, doing almost all of the child rearing myself.

The cost of processed foods is not only extreme in comparison to whole foods, the hidden costs implied above make it borderline evil to continue to consume processed foods and drinks. For example, compare the real cost of one bag of potato chips to a fresh bag of potatoes, cooked at home, by following the potato from farm to post consumption.

The humble potato is transported to a manufacturing plant where many other resources, chemicals, and fossil fuel and hydroelectric energies are used to convert the potato into chips. Fossil fuel use adds to global warming and pollution. Hydroelectric power requires the damming of natural waterways, causing severe environmental damage and unsuccessful relocation of people and other species. The process spurts out toxins into the air, water and land. The plastic packaging for the chips requires manufacture, doing further environmental damage. The product is then boxed, using wood or plastic (petroleum) products, and transported to stores using more petroleum. The box is generally discarded at the retail outlet and the package around the chips is generally discarded at home. The discards cost in the millions yearly for disposal out of sight, though never out of the common biosphere. As stated previously, discarded garbage is buried, burned, or shipped, adding to environmental toxins. All the manufacturing processes and transportation of resources add to global warming and climate change.

ASIDE: please don't tell me we can ship our waste into space. The environmental and fiscal costs alone would be astronomical. Grow up and stop pooping in the only pair of pants we have! End of rant!

Having done multiple amounts of environmental damage in producing, transporting, shipping and discarding the waste, the consumed potato chip continues to cause harm. All the toxins consumed upon ingesting the potato chips are eventually eliminated and flushed away, only to contaminate the shared communal waters. Not to mention there was no nutritional value to the potato chips, and a steady diet of this type of processed food produces ill health, straining the health care system, giving further impetus to right wing governments to privatize health care.

On the other hand, if the bag of potatoes were prepared into nutritious food it could feed a family of four easily, though a diet of just potatoes is not recommended. If eaten with the skin there is no waste, and considerably more nutrition. The cost of a pound of potato chips is about ten times the cost of a pound of organic, locally grown potatoes.

This line of reasoning applies to all non-whole foods; pre-prepared convenience foods, virtually all prepared snacks, candy bars, soft drinks, sports drinks, specialty coffees and teas, most cereals, deli meats, most condiments, and almost every thing served at a fast food outlet. Our children do not need to be poisoned for the sake of adult convenience and brainwashing by the Advertising Apostles. The diet that children receive from the Western Minded adult is in effect child abuse through serious neglect. Child abuse in any other form is legally punishable, but this form is not even recognized as such. If poisoning children is not a crime of abuse then the Western Minded ought to reconsider having any children.

A well-nourished child performs much better in school, sports, and in life. Many of the Western Minded pay inordinately large sums for private schooling for their children, and yet they can not give enough of themselves to prepare a nourishing breakfast and lunch for their children. Without appropriate and adequate nourishment children consistently fail to do well, and suffer from more illness later in life than children raised on good, wholesome, homemade food.

Children need fresh fruit and vegetables, whole grains and natural cereals, limited amount of protein and a few other essentials. Feed them the fruit and give them water, not juice. How ridiculous is it that children are given artificially flavored fruit leather and artificially flavoured drinks, while furniture polish and toilet cleaners contains real lemon or orange juice? If you must give them something other than water, then make sure it is 100% real juice, not a fruit cocktail, or a fruit drink. If humans really had needed sports drinks then one is totally baffled to explain how pioneers and pirates had survived without them. Stop advertisers from colonizing your minds to gain control of your hard earned money, and from killing your children as collateral damage!

Basically, more than minimally processed foods and drinks are toxic waste, and they contribute to many of the ills facing humanity. Most of the heavily processed foods are industrially farmed before processing. Industrially farmed food contains a small fraction of the essential nutrients available only fifty years ago in food grown naturally. It also contains far greater levels of fats, salts and toxins than are healthy for growing young bodies. The conversion of whole foods to toxic waste uses our limited fossil fuels, the control of which is the major reason for current wars, and the overuse of which is the major reason for global warming.

With greater demand for fresh, whole foods the supply will follow. Pound for pound organic, whole foods are cheaper and more nutritious than industrially farmed processed foods. Organic farming replenishes soils, making artificial fertilizers, pesticides, and herbicides totally unnecessary. The manufacture of these three is another environmental pollutant. Genetically modified foods require specific fertilizers, pesticides, and herbicides, and in the end do much more harm to humans and other Life. They are of financial benefit only, and even that only to the corporations that hold monopolies and patents on the G.M.O.s.

Most of the processed foods contain at least one of corn, soy, sugar, or peanuts. The farming of these is heavily subsidized compared to healthier, whole, organic foods. Also, many Majority World countries export these crops in exchange for aid. This leaves them with little or no land to grow food for them-selves, and we use their crops to convert real food into toxic waste for our children to consume.

Now for the complaints, "Yeah but I don't have time to cook fresh food every day." Firstly, where are your priorities? What is more important than the health and wellbeing of your children? Secondly, fresh food costs much less, and less is needed for adequate nourishment. Thirdly, since your family will be healthier, your medical costs will be less. Fourthly, whole foods can require less energy to cook since more is eaten fresh, lowering your hydro bill. With a few other changes, which will be introduced in subsequent pages, the average family can save thousands of dollars yearly, and be able to afford to have parents at home more often to prepare real food for a loved family.

It bears repeating that understanding all the above global connections and still choosing to consume non-minimally processed foods and drinks is an evil act of a lazy people, that loves convenience more than the innocent young.

See chart #3 page 88
See chart #4 page 93

CHART #3: ON POTATO CHIPS

AT THE VERY LEAST MANUFACTURE OF THESE REQUIRES TRANSPORT, MANUFACTURING FACILITY, RETAILERS, CROPS, PACKAGING, ADVERTISING, WASTE DISPOSAL, AND OTHER INGREDIENT.THESE IN TURN REQUIRE OTHER RESOURCES WHICH NEED STILL OTHERS, AND SUBSEQUENTLY DO THE FOLLOWING SOCIAL AND GLOBAL DAMAGE.

TRANSPORT

a) fossil fuels◊ extraction from the Earth ----------- ◊ Environmental damage to land, sea and air, promotes wars

◊ energy----------- ◊ Environmental damage to land, sea and air, promotes wars

◊ machinery----------- ◊ Manufacture damages environment and depletes resources

b) roads ◊machinery ----------- ◊ Manufacture damages environment and depletes resources

◊ fossil fuels----------- ◊ Adds to green house gasses, climate change, and global warming

◊ land----------- ◊ Effects natural pathways, increased road kill

◊ vehicles ◊factories----------- ◊ Manufacture of these adds to environmental pollutants

◊ fossil fuels----------- ◊ Extraction and use increase global warming

◊ metal, plastic, wood,fabric, glass...----------- ◊ All created in factories, causing increased pollution

MANUFACTURE

a) factories ◊ building----------- ◊ Construction requires materials made in factories

◊ equipment----------- ◊ All equipment is made in factories

b) energy ◊ fossil fuels ----------- ◊ Factories run on fossil fuels and hydroelectric energy,

      & hydroelectric energy ---------------- ◊ Increase global warming and climate change

c) ingredients ◊ see below---------------- ◊ See below under "Other Ingredients "

RETAIL FACILITY

a) building ◊ land   ---------------- ◊ For every building there is a decrease in green space and clean air

b) equipment   ---------------- ◊ All are made in factories, increasing pollution, depleting resources

c) parking lot ◊ land   ---------------- ◊ Every building / parking lot decreases green space and clean air

d) energy for operations ◊ fossil fuels ---------------- ◊ Extraction and use add to global warming, climate change, and warfare

                        ◊ hydroelectric ---------------- ◊ Damming of waterways causes environmental damage, and relocation

POTATOES

a) if organically farmed

      ◊ land ---------------- ◊ Soil nutrients are replenished

      ◊ water---------------- ◊ No toxin contamination of ground water

      ◊ sun ---------------- ◊ Nothing to negatively effect greenhouse formation

      ◊ air ---------------- ◊ No toxic off gassing

      ◊ natural fertilizer, pesticide,

      herbicide, fungicides ---------------- ◊ Replenish essential soil nutrients, increase nutritional value, which is destroyed when transformed to chips

      ◊ labour intensive, less farm machinery --- ◊ Manual labour does little damage in comparison to farm machinery

b) if chemically farmed

      ◊ land ---------------- ◊ Soil nutrients are depleted

      ◊ water---------------- ◊ Chemical toxins contaminate the communal ground water

◊ sun ----------------------- ◊ Manufacture, packaging and shipping add to greenhouse gasses

◊air----------------------- ◊ All add to air pollution in their manufacture, packaging, and shipping

◊ chemical fertilizers, pesticides,

herbicides, fungicides ----------- ◊ Deplete soil nutrients, and add toxins to potatoes

◊ farm machine intensive---------- ◊ Much more environmental damage than labour intensive organic farming

OTHER INGREDIENTS

a) flavours / colours   ◊ chemicals----------- ◊ Made in factories, adding to pollution, depleting natural resources

◊ energy----------- ◊ Fossil fuel and hydroelectric, increasing global warming and pollution

◊ factories ----------- ◊ Produce an increase in pollution

b) oils   ◊ crops ----------- ◊ All the same damage as done by growing non organic potatoes, and deprive Majority World farmers of land to feed their families

◊ factories ----------- ◊ Add to pollution

◊ energy----------- ◊ Fossil fuel and hydroelectric, add to global warming and pollution

c) preservatives   ◊ chemicals----------- ◊ All are made in factories, adding to pollution, depleting resources

◊ factories ----------- ◊ Add to pollution

◊ energy----------- ◊ Fossil fuel and hydroelectric, add to global warming and pollution

PACKAGING

a) factory ◊ building   ◊ see above ----------- ◊ Reduce green space and clean air, deplete resources, & increase pollution

◊ energy ◊ see above---------- ◊ Fossil fuel and hydroelectric, add to global warming and pollution

◊ equipment/manufacturing plants –◊ see above ◊ All made in factories, adding to global warming, pollution, resource depletion

b) transport   ◊ see transportation above -------- ◊ See above

c) energy   ◊ fossil fuel   ◊ see above -------- ◊ Add to global warming, climate change, pollution, wars

         ◊ hydroelectric ◊ see above-------- ◊ Destroy environment, and increase species extinction

d) petroleum for plastic packaging------------------------------------ ◊ Control of which is the cause of many wars today

e) trees for paper packaging --- ◊ Reduce air quality, increase siltation of waters, destroy habitat

ADVERTISING

a) agency   ◊ building   ◊ see above------------------------ ◊ Reduces green space, air quality and natural resources

b) clever people   ◊ trained at taxpayers expense-------------- ◊ Wastes talent for ill gotten gains

c) appropriate resources   ------------------------------- ◊ Depleting natural resources

d) media   ◊ print, audio, visual, electronic------------------- ◊ All requiring resources, and adding to brain washing

WASTE DISPOSAL

a) from manufacturing

         ◊ created in manufacturing------------- ◊ Depletion of natural resources, increase in pollution and global warming

         ◊ transport to disposal site ---------- ◊ Depletion of natural resources, increase in pollution and global warming

b) from retail outlet   ◊ same as above ----------------- ◊ Depletion of natural resources, increase in pollution and global warming

c) from consumer   ◊ same as above --------------------- ◊ Depletion of natural resources, increase in pollution and global warming

IN SUMMARY, THESE ARE THE NET RESULTS OF THE CONVENIENCE OF CONSUMING PROCCESSED FOODS AND DRINKS:

1   They contain virtually no nutrients for a human body.

2   The artificial colours & flavours are harmful to health.

3   The extent of the environmental damage done by the sum of all the processes has the following effects;
~ increase in rates of cancer
~ an increase in respiratory ailments
~ an increase in green house gasses
~ an increase in global warming
~ an increase in rate of climate change
~ an increase in extreme, unpredictable weather
~ a decrease in natural resources
~ an increased need for petroleum & its products, to further fuel warfare and also its environmental impact

4   Disposal of all the waste created pollutes the ground water, the air, the land, and negatively effects the Sun's rays, and effects the wellbeing of The Majority World.

5   Digested toxic chemicals are eventually flushed down the drain and contaminate the communal ground water.

6   More medical services are needed due to poor diet and due to environment related illnesses, placing a strain on health care, giving more impetus to privatize health care.

7   Waste of valuable land in converting good crops to toxic waste, while millions go hungry.

ONE MAY SUBSTITUTE ANY OTHER PROCESSED FOOD (CANDIES, CAKES, COOKIES, CHOCOLATES, FRUIT BARS, PRE-PACKAGED SNACKS, TV DINNERS, ...) OR DRINK (POP, SPORTSDRINKS, CHRYSTALS, NOVELTY COFFEES AND TEAS...) FOR POTATO CHIPS AND ARRIVE AT THE SAME CONCLUSION OF THE INSANITY OF MAKING, INGESTING, AND FEEDING CHILDREN THESE TOXINS.

CHART #4: ON UNPROCESSED POTATOES

A) ORGANICALLY FARMED POTATOES REQUIRE THE FOLLOWING RESOURCES AND HAVE THE LISTED EFFECTS.

a) **land** ◊ replenish essential soil nutrients

b) **water** ◊ no danger of contamination to ground water

c) **air** ◊ no off gassing of toxins

d) **sun** ◊ no negative effect on the greenhouse gasses

e) **natural fertilizers, herbicides, pesticides, fungicides** ◊ replenish soil nutrients, increase nutrition in potato

f) **farm equipment** ◊ less is used than chemical farming, it is more labor intensive, so much more planet friendly

◊ manufacture◊depletes natural resources, adds to pollution, global warming, climate change, species extinction, increases ill health, adds to causes of wars

◊ requires fossil fuels ◊ adds to pollution, global warming, climate change, ocean pollution, species extinction, and causes of war over resources

g) **transport to buyer** ◊ at source ◊ perhaps a little more damage than going to retail chain

◊ at farmers market ◊ same damage as going to retail chain, perhaps

◊ at retail chain ◊ considerable environmental damage due to trucking

When appropriately cooked and ingested the potato confers many healthful benefits, in particular if is cooked with the skin. Uncooked skin can become nutritious fertilizer for flower and vegetable beds.

B) INDUSTRIALLY OR NON-ORGANICALLY FARMED POTATOES REQUIRE THE FOLLOWING RESOURCES AND THE HAVE THE LISTED EFFECTS:

a) **land** ◊ soil is deleted of essential nutrients

b) **water** ◊ ground water is contaminated

c) **air**   ◊ off gassing of chemicals used

d) **sun**   ◊ manufacture of chemical fertilizers, pesticides and herbicides adds to green house gasses

e) **artificial fertilizers, pesticides fungicides and herbicides**

◊ deplete soil nutrients

◊ their manufacture creates pollution of the land, water and air

◊ manufacture of packaging for these creates similar pollution

◊ transport of these creates more pollution

◊ disposal of packaging creates more pollution

f) **farm equipment**

◊ much more is used than organic farming, it is more chemical intensive, so much more harmful

◊ manufacture◊depletes natural resources, adds to pollution, global warming, climate change, species extinction, increases ill health, adds to causes of wars

◊ requires fossil fuels ◊ adds to pollution, global warming, climate change, ocean pollution, species extinction, and causes of war over resources

g) **transport to buyer**

◊ at source ◊ perhaps a little more damage than going to retail chain

◊ at farmers market ◊ same damage as going to retail chain, perhaps

◊ at retail chain ◊ considerable environmental damage due to trucking'

When appropriately cooked and ingested this potato has about half the nutrients of an organically grown potato, contains harmful chemicals, and much higher levels of salt and fats than an organic potato.

IN THE PLACE OF "POTATO" ONE COULD SUBSTITUTE ANY PRODUCE OR CROP AND ARRIVE AT THE SAME CONCLUSION OF THE SANITY OF INGESTING ORGANIC, WHOLE FOODS, EATEN CLOSE TO THEIR NATURAL STATE, WHICH ARE LOCAL AND SEASONAL. THE SAME IS TRUE OF DRINKING WATER INSTEAD OF ANY ONE OF THE HUNDREDS OF PROCESSED DRINKS.KNOWING ALL THIS, IT IS SURE INSANITY TO CONTINUE TO CONSUME PROCESSED FOODS AND DRINKS IN THE MASSIVE QUANTITIES IT IS DONE DAILY AT PRESENT.

SOLUTION #3: USE ITEMS MADE OF NATURAL THINGS IN CARING FOR CHILDREN
BECAUSE IT WILL:

~ improve the quality of the environment,
~ reduce your child's, and your own ecological footprints,
~ slow down global warming and climate change,
~ reduce armed conflict, and W.M.D. amassment,
~ relieve poverty in the Majority World,
~ improve the quality of life for all,
~ **and SAVE MONEY.**

HOW IS THAT POSSIBLE?

Wet Wipes, disposable diapers, paper towels, oversized designer strollers and carriages, are some of the many consumables the Western Minded purchase for their infants. The manufacture of disposable towels and diapers pours toxins into the environment. The chemicals used in both are harmful to baby skin, leaching into their bodies, giving them a head start in accumulating cancer causing toxins. The final disposal of both creates toxic sludge in landfills, or acid rain after incineration, or environmental pollut-ants where ever else they are shipped for waste management.

About two-dozen cotton diapers and two-dozen cotton face cloths are ample supplies for one baby. Natural fibers like silk, cotton, wool, hemp do not require the chemical detergents that have been created for synthetic fibers. Chemical detergents are another petroleum product, as are synthetic fabrics. When cotton diapers and face cloths are washed with planet friendly soap, in a full load, the damage to the environment is minimal in com-parison.

One of the most inhumane habits of the Western Minded parent is the obsessive use of plastic buckets to contain a baby for most of the baby's waking hours. This excessive use of convertible car/carry/sleep seats is extremely harmful to normal emotional development. Tribal people, and those too poor to afford these plastic buckets, know the value of human touch to healthy development. Western psychologists have ample studies to state conclusively that babies need a great deal more human touch than is given by the Western Minded. Aside from the emotional damage, these are just more petroleum products contributing to global injustice issues already outlined.

Most of the other paraphernalia that the Western Minded buy and use is made with petroleum products, in Majority World sweat shops, under no labour or environmental regulations. This paraphernalia includes massive strollers, loaded diaper bags, and plastic toys. Each item of plastic paraphernalia is another petroleum product, emitting off gasses, supplying babies with more of the toxins needed to create cancer in later life.

Plastic bottles are no less harmful. The warming of milk in plastic bottles using a microwave not only destroys the limited nutrients in baby formula, heating the plastic releases toxic gasses, and leaches hormones into the milk. Both of these contribute to a build up of carcinogens in innocent babies.

Bedding, clothing and furnishings made of synthetic materials require petroleum products, off gas toxins, and continue to add to baby's store of cancer causing agents.

Use natural, and fewer items to ensure a healthier life for all, peace and security for all, save a lot of money in the process, work less outside the home, allowing more quality time with your loved ones.

Are we willing to give up your addiction to convenience? Are the children worth it?

SOLUTION #4: PROVIDE CHILDREN WITH A LIMITED AMOUNT OF "STUFF", MADE OF NATURAL MATERIALS

BECAUSE IT WILL:

~ make them more secure,

~ promote their creativity,

~ reduce environmental damage,

~ slow down global warming and climate change,

~ promote human rights,

~ reduce armed conflict and W.M.D. amassment,

~ reduce reasons for illegal occupations,

~ improve family life,

~ improve health,

~ make universal health care a greater reality,

~ **and SAVE MONEY.**

HOW IS THAT POSSIBLE?

Children of the Western Minded have rooms filled with totally unnecessary junk, mostly made of plastics, which are petroleum products. Wars are being fought over control of petroleum, and the shipping of petroleum is destroying the oceans. The junk is not limited to non-essentials; it includes all the synthetic clothing, footwear, sports gear, electronic gadgets, accessories, toiletries, bedding, furnishings and even the interior decorating.

Once again, almost all of these are manufactured in the sweat-shops of the Majority World, creating havoc with the environment, violating human rights, stocking carcinogens in children's bodies, and costing a lot of money. Material wealth for the few has only created the conditions for poor health, global injustice, and for wars that continue to plague the many.

It is not a sign of love or good parenting to fill a child's life with "stuff". It is more often the sign of a weak parent, brainwashed by the Apostles of Advertising, peer pressure, and the nurtured whining of their children. It is a true act of courage and love to give of yourself and not of your bank account.

Fill your child's life with life skills, creativity, imagination, love, and community service. Gadgets, T.V.s, computers, video games and other electronic wonders have not produced better quality, happier adults. In fact, we now have more gross numbers of dysfunctional adults than ever before the electronic revolution. What is more, the microchips in most of the gadgets and toys are made under conditions where hundreds lose their eyesight and/or other faculties, while working under the few safety measures available to Majority World workers.

Children just might need a computer to get ahead in schooling. They do not need a computer to get educated. They need motivation, modeling, and methods of utilizing the masses of information obtained via computers. They do not need any of the myriads of material items with which we clutter their lives. They need us to model for them all that we say we want them, and the world to be. The less wealthy do this much better than those of us with money and our Western Minded attitudes of entitlement.

Fewer clothes, shoes, and accessories of natural fibers, of a higher quality, made under union labels, and costing a little more will teach both the parent and the child to respect the possessions they have, to take care of them, and to acquire fewer of them. At present most of these are synthetic, petroleum products, made in sweatshops by children of the descendants of the formerly colonized, labouring without any safety standards. Buying local and/ or union made guarantees fair wages, especially to the bulk of the garment workers in our western nations, who are mostly underpaid immigrant women.

Is a Western Minded person's child worth more than a Majority World child? In terms of intrinsic value, one would say absolutely not! In terms of usefulness to humanity the Majority World child appears to be of much more use.

Provide children with constructive materials when young, and with community service when a little older. Teach them and share cooking, cleaning, laundry, chores, and conversation with them. Begin at the very start, not after a few years. Develop yours, and their creativities together. Model a love of learning, and of service to those we love. Any fool can give "stuff"; it is the wise who freely give of themselves.

If schools are educating children, processed food manufactures are feeding them, malls are watching over them, electronic gadgets are entertaining them, and outside help is managing their home and yard, then what exactly is it that parents are doing towards children's upbringing? Earning money to pay for all that, you say! Stop and reflect on this. How ludicrous is that?

By eliminating toxic foods and drinks, and the junk and clutter from children's lives we can create a better world for all in many, many global ways. Do we have the courage to go against the tide and do right by the children of today and tomorrow?

CHAPTER EIGHT:

SCHOOLING AND EDUCATION

No one can reveal to you aught but that which already lies deep within the
Dawning of your own knowledge.
The teacher… gives not of their wisdom but rather of … their lovingness.
If they are wise they do not bid you enter the house of their wisdom, but
Rather lead you to the threshold of your own mind…
For the vision of one person lends not its wings to another's.

Kahlil Gibran

The current model of our educational system is very recent in the overall history of humanity. Long ago families passed their time in small communities: living, learning, and dying in natural rhythms and cycles. Learning came through being and doing. In those times universal health care was a natural balance of the physical, emotional, intellectual and spiritual selves, when the economy was the land, when the grocery store was the forest, when the group took precedence over the self, when there was no word for greed or war, and when reverence for all of creation was in vogue. When these things were then there was **Education; that is, the balanced development of the emotional, physical, intellectual and spiritual interdependent parts of being human.**

"Education"; "the art of developing and cultivating the various physical, intellectual, aesthetic, and moral faculties; instruction and discipline; nurture." As typically defined by industrialized civilizations, this definition fails to overtly encompass the spiritual and emotional aspects of being human, and it fails to address the aims of education. For, without a larger, universal life enhancing purpose, education is merely a disjoint activity, irrelevant to Life and the living of it. It is just schooling.

Preceding the institutionalization of schooling by colonial powers education was not a disjoint activity for the indulgence of the privileged, with little or no enhancement of Life. Education was conducted continuously at the side of members of a community as a child was reared to acquire **skills needed to be human, skills that made a person literate in Life: such as procurement of food, shelter, safety, belonging, meaning and wellbeing within a community, without placing excessive strain on the natural systems.** Education meant learning to be human within the milieu of relationships that spanned three or four generations. It meant equity, security, and spiritual connectedness for all; it meant knowing one's place of infinite worth in the interdependent systems of the Cosmos. Education's only aim was to determine what it meant to be human and how best to nurture that. The entire membership of the community was the learner and the teacher.

The earliest schooling institutions of the European colonizers were generally religious in nature, content, available only to men training for the priesthood, and they were very limited in their conception of an educated person, or the purpose of education. Eventually they evolved into institutions for the sons of the wealthy and powerful, who in turn became political, military, economic, academic and social powers, viewing the world through the lens of the value system inherent within the religious philosophies of the institutions; philosophies that promoted domination, exploitation, competition, social Darwinism, and a demonization of the Other. Soon other academic notables, scientists and philosophers elevated this value system further by introducing the viewpoint that the universe was mechanical in nature, reducible to its parts, and entirely for the benefit of "man" who was apart from the natural world, and superiour to it.

Of the four intertwined parts of being human the intellectual and the physical became associated with maleness and the masculine, and the emotional and spiritual with femaleness and the feminine. Since the religious institutions abhorred anything feminine as vile, evil and untrustworthy, of course the values that developed for schooling males excluded anything of the feminine. This abhorrence and exclusion of the feminine continues to this day and its effects are dealt with in a little more detail in a subsequent chapter.

In a short time institutions for schooling of this model spread their influence over the entire face of the planet as a corollary to colonization. In the wake of the havoc of colonization these institutions taught their fragmented curriculum, with no regard to what it meant to live as humans. They created several successive generations of people, in the millions, who lacked the ability to procure food, shelter, safety, belonging, meaning and spiritual wellbeing within a community without placing excessive stain on the natural systems.

Today the people created by this model frequently graduate into chronological adulthood without having been nurtured into being one significant component within a complex, multi-layered, dynamic, interconnected, interdependent set of natural and human made systems. They are short changed by cultures that grant great status to a "higher education" if it is obtained in a sterile institution, devoid of contact with the natural world systems. It is no surprise that millions fail to find belonging, safety, and spiritual wellbeing following so many centuries of believing in the superiority to, and separation from the natural world. The abundance of insecurity created by our institutions of schooling has been filled with greed, fear, consumption, despair, abuse, short-sightedness, and distrust.

The model of education inflicted upon the world during colonization has largely failed to cultivate the skills for being human; it schools through fragmentation of the Cosmos into parcels of knowledge, whose availability is often differentiated by age, gender, race, religion, socioeconomic level, geographic location, and sexual orientation. The belief of this model is that one is being prepared with survival skills for the human engineered world systems, and that these skills will lead to gainful employment. What remains un-understood is that the human engineered systems are ultimately dependent on the natural systems of the Cosmos, and that survival skills for the former invariably fail if survival skills for the latter are not a first priority. Namely, the being human skills stated previously.

Even the aim of teaching for employment goes unmet, since current workplace requirements demand more than The Three R's of the schooling of the past. Currently, communication skills, creativity, critical thinking, adaptability, group effectiveness, and knowing how to, not just what to learn, rank near the top for workplace requirements. These are not taught since they cannot be easily measured to satisfy the powers that control the school budgets, and the learning of these would inevitably lead to the asking of the hard questions. Furthermore, teachers can only teach what they know, and the institutions for higher learning do not prepare teachers fully for teaching more than The Three R's. Teachers of today are also time strapped with the added burden of having to be surrogate parents, counselors, drug awareness experts, sex educators, road safety instructors, fund raisers, conflict mediators, medication dispensers, ….

This model of schooling has operated on the belief that "knowing" is an empirical activity established by earlier academics, scientists and philosophers, all the while denying and devaluing others' ways of "knowing". This has limited our knowledge pool and placed us on the brink of extinction. Colonization marginalized, relocated, assimilated, romanticized, patronized and, or exterminated all groups who had had Education. They were dismissed as barbarians, heathens, primitives, illiterate, naïve, and lower forms of life that had to be raised to an acceptable standard through the religion based schooling of the invaders.

Sadly, families in former colonies now make heroic efforts to obtain a good education for their children by sending them great distances to foreign cultures, in the belief that this will guarantee economic security, and thus food, clothing, and shelter. All too often this schooling does not reflect, nor is consistent with, the understanding the offspring would have had on the nature of reality and on being human, thereby creating personal and interpersonal conflict, along with the breakdown of the family, and traditional values and systems.

Virtually the only model of schooling available to us today promotes the imparting of values of fragmentation, domination, competition, exploitation, mechanization, acquisition and consumption, and develops monoculture-ism. This model must undergo a radical transformation if issues of peace, human rights, sustainable and equitable development, and environment are to find positive resolutions that lead to the enhancement of Life, and of being human.

It would be ludicrous, and generally undesirable, to suggest a return to models and methodologies of long ago, for our species has evolved and its needs for survival at this moment in time are very different from those earlier times. In those times we were not faced with nuclear armament amassment in sufficient quantity to obliterate all signs of life in Earth's biosphere. We were not faced with fear of our own Sun's rays, or of the acid in our rain, or of the toxins in our water, food, soil and air. We face gross poverty in numbers greater than ever; uncontrollable epidemic diseases; escalating deforestation and desertification; global warming and its catastrophic consequences; frequent famines; rising rates of species extinction; entire nations of people endangered through genocide; scores of wars; billions of women, children, persons of colour, persons of diverse beliefs and sexual persuasion being abused, tortured and/or persecuted.

We must educate people to fully appreciate and take responsible action from their own place of infinite worth in the interconnected, dynamic systems of the Cosmos. It is the lack of awareness of this element that is the root cause of much of what ails humanity and its home. And it is precisely this element that is needed if the global model for schooling is to be metamorphosed into a model for Education.

Our educational system needs to reflect, and be consistent with, the consistently similar findings on the nature of reality as reported by at least three independent sources. Ancient texts of Eastern mysticism, ancient oral traditions of First Peoples, and modern theoretical physicists and cosmologists all assert the same truth; every phenomenon in existence is made of the same universal building blocks, and is inextricably linked by dynamic systems to every other phenomenon in existence. With a common understanding of the nature of reality, of our common cosmic heritage, and a model for educating that reflects this reality we would make considerable progress towards achieving a just and peaceful world, for all of Life.

SOLUTION # 5: LOBBY YOUR SCHOOLBOARD TO EMPLOY TEACHERS WHO ARE TRAINED GLOBAL EDUCATORS, IN THEORY, PRACTICE, AND EXAMPLE BECAUSE IT WILL:

~ cultivate more balanced, secure people,
~ help to solve all the world's problems,
~ create peace and harmony for all of Life,
~ and **SAVE MONEY.**

HOW IS THIS POSSIBLE?

Global education is a philosophical movement and educational methodology, not a separate discipline. It is a way of teaching; in fact, it is a way of life. It teaches the links between the issues of peace, human rights, sustainable development, and environment. It links all the global issues to our individual lifestyles. The methodology of global education can easily accomplish all this using existing resources, using a great deal less of them, and using them in a much more critical, analytical manner. It dramatically furthers the aim of raising a more secure society that is truly educated, not just schooled, able to live fulfilling lives without placing excessive strains on the natural systems of our only biosphere. Promoting greater simplicity, this model helps create citizens who have a lesser interest in material consumption, therefore, saving money.

This author's life has been devoted to being, living, teaching, and modeling the global citizenship way of life, with varying degrees of success. This entire work is a guided walk through understanding the inextricable links between peace, human rights, development, environment and individual life styles. And so it ought to be self-evident why the Global Education model is the kind of model we should cultivate in all schools of the current Western Minded model.

SOLUTION #6: LEARN ABOUT AND TEACH YOUR CHILDREN WHAT IS CURRENTLY KNOWN ABOUT THE NATURE OF REALITY

BECAUSE IT WILL:

~ relieve some religious tensions,
~ provide a healthier paradigm for interpersonal relationships,
~ develop compassion,
~ improve the health of our biosphere,
~ reduce global warming,
~ curb climate change,
~ reduce the number of excuses for wars, armed conflict and W.M.D. amassment,
~ and **SAVE MONEY**

HOW IS THAT POSSIBLE?

To learn about the nature of reality and of the universe does not conflict with any religious beliefs. Those that would fear monger that it is are the insecure leadership, struggling to keep their tenuous control over the minds of their flock. In the deepest, most mystical, spiritual aspects of all faiths one finds the same assertions: everything is interconnected and interdependent, and that to be fully human means living in congruence with this.

It is to the economic benefit of the organized religion industry to keep groups suspicious and apart. Firstly, by instilling the belief that the poor, underprivileged will always be with us, and that charity and alms will buy a better afterlife, organized religions are able to amass fortunes, a small portion of which is used for charitable work. The underlying causes for why charity is needed are rarely addressed. Secondly, it is easier to control a group if it is lead to believe there is a common enemy. Thirdly, for the masses to learn a bigger truth would shatter the very foundations of several faiths, and render the institutions impotent.

It takes courage to search for a bigger truth. It is not something a lazy mind would want to tackle. Though, once it has been done, one cannot help but behave with more reverence for all of Life, with more compassion for every living thing, including the largest living organism in our solar system, the Earth's biosphere. The excessive strain on the natural systems is diminished, consumption of non-essentials decrease, thereby improving the environment, reducing global warming and climate change. In consuming less "stuff" money is saved, resources are conserved and the need for wars over control of resources is reduced.

SOLUTION #7: TEACH OUR BOYS "GIRL" THINGS BECAUSE IT WILL:

~ reduce misogyny, and violence against females and the feminine,
~ reduce warfare, militarization, and W.M.D. amassment,
~ increase cooperation and security,
~ improve the environment,
~ decrease global warming,
~ curb climate change,
~ address world poverty,
~ fund cures for A.I.D.S.,
~ and **SAVE MONEY.**

HOW IS THIS POSSIBLE?

For many centuries females and the feminine have been exploited, abused, dominated, devalued, and generally held responsible for everything that is considered wrong with society. We now consider it barbaric that in times long ago, for a female to be considered human she had had to pretend to be a male. In the past authors, physicians, saints, popes, enlightened females of Eastern and Western faiths, artists, scientists, inventors, and others have had to pose as males to fulfill their dreams. It was barbaric then, and yet today, we have made zero progress in accepting the feminine and femaleness as having any more intrinsic value than in the past.

We have gone to extraordinary lengths to have our girls interested in "boy" subjects in schools, sports, professions, trades, and in universities, in fact, in life in general. We have encouraged our girls to dress like boys. We have made way for girls in the armed forces. We have created leagues for female athletes playing traditionally male sports. We have even created porn for females in the same genre as has existed for males. We have devoted centuries to telling females they can do anything a male can do, and indeed told them to do it or be considered losers. So, of course females have learned to do and be all that was traditionally male domain, along with what was their traditionally female domain. In the process becoming proficient at most things male and female. In the mean time our males appear to have become redundant, able to fire on only half as many cylinders as their female counterparts.

The result has led to some very serious consequences for all of humanity. In giving encouragement to females to become more like males we have done humanity a double disservice. Firstly, we have reinforced the value that maleness and the masculine are superior to the feminine and femaleness, and that being these are goals worthy of aspiration. Secondly, we have reinforced a lack of value for the feminine and femaleness, and also that no one worthy should aspire to it. Both of these are the root of the injustices inflicted upon women and girls, and blatant evidence of the misogyny that is endemic on all continents.

Had we expended even a fraction of the time, energy and re-sources to encourage our boys to take interest in becoming more like girls, we would have far better balanced men today. There would be greater understanding and harmony between the gen-ders, less violence against women and girls, less exploitation of the weak, and of the biosphere, and less need for control of resources and militarization.

One can hear a very loud chorus of both men and women ex-claiming, **"That is a ridiculous idea!"**

We must ask ourselves why it seems like such a ridiculous idea to have boys and men become more like women in their traditional roles? The answer: because society sees little value in the femi-nine. If a boy expresses any interest in the feminine, other than sexual, he is mocked and tormented with homophobic taunts. And yet, no girl receives homophobic bullying for wearing pants, studying engineering, playing sports, or fixing the lawn mower. She may, on the other hand, end up murdered in a massacre of women simply for being ..."a fucking feminist..." studying engi-neering; but she will not be subject to homophobia as a boy often is if he studies home economics, nursing, or dance. You and I perpetuate the devaluing of the feminine by not giving our boys the same opportunities to develop traditional feminine attributes as we do when we encourage our girls to develop more tradition-ally male values.

There is always the possibility that it has been out of necessity that females have had to become more adept at evolving the male-fe-male balance. Perhaps too many males have absented themselves from family and home responsibilities, for too long, and the slack has had to be picked up by women.

Misogyny rears its ugly head in many manifestations, not the least of which is the tormenting of males displaying feminine char-acteristics. It seems to be irrelevant whether or not they are homosexuals, it is assumed to be the case. It is falsely believed that A.I.D.S. is an infliction of homosexual males only, as a punishment from a horribly vindictive, mean spirited god. And so, misogyny, manifest as homophobia, in addition to the religious edict against the use of condoms, has placed the access to prevention and to treatment for A.I.D.S. relatively low on our priorities. In elevating the status of the feminine we develop much better balanced people, who are able to be more empathetic, and do right by women, homosexuals, and the millions with A.I.D.S.

When boys become better balanced they do better in school. Currently they are lagging well behind girls due to their lack of feminine skills development; that is, lack of developing skills to use both sides of their brain. Not only that, they become more respectful of females, resolve conflicts in more peaceful ways, show less aggressive behaviour, are more compassionate and caring, and less competitive. All this translates into a diminished need to control people, events and resources, leading to a healthier environment, fewer wars, and a more equitable sharing of the Earths bounty.

SOLUTION #8; KEEP CORPORATIONS OUT OF SCHOOLS, COLLEGES, AND UNIVERSITIES IF THERE ARE ANY STRINGS ATTACHED

BECAUSE IT WILL:

~ ensure a better quality education,
~ protect national sovereignty,
~ improve the student's wellbeing,
~ reduce Majority world poverty,
~ improve the environment,
~ reduce global warming,
~ curb climate change,
~ reduce resource depletion,
~ and thus the causes of wars, and amassment of W.M.D.,
~ and **SAVE MONEY.**

HOW IS THIS POSSIBLE

The #1 mandate of a corporation is to make profits for its share-holders. Fair enough!

Institutions for educating the young are not places for advertising, selling brands or controlling curriculum content. Students do not need the "stuff" promised in order to become truly educated. They do not need the latest of any "stuff" to learn. The most brilliant, already well schooled minds heading the research labs in Western universities and hospitals, and heading various university departments and industries have been trained in, and then poached from, India, China and a few other Majority World countries. Cuba ranks amongst the highest in the world for best trained doctors and most advanced scientists. How is it that educational systems of such poor countries are providing the academic, scientific, economic and medical leaders for the wealthiest nations? Because they do not allow themselves into being mind controlled by profiteers. They know the greatest learning and teaching aids are already within us.

In not allowing corporations control of our schools and universities we can keep education a sovereign affair, creating culturally appropriate education to suit our own priorities. Much of what corporations wish to sell in schools is highly processed food and drinks, and cheap, petroleum based goods made in Majority World sweatshops. The links between these and the other consequences listed above have been made previously.

Is the suffering of the many worth the schooling of the few?

SOLUTION #9: STOP FUNDRAISING FOR SCHOOLS BY SELLING JUNK FOOD, PETROLEUM BASED TRINKETS, AND OTHER NON-ESSENTIAL ITEMS LIKE GIFT WRAP

BECAUSE IT WILL:

The reason against and the extent of the damage done to all of Life by all of these has already been explained.

Furthermore, in Solution #7 it was shown more "stuff" does not guarantee a better education for those that already have "stuff". What makes the difference is what happens in the homes of the students. If parents value learning and model this, then students do much better in school and life, and teachers in schools are only secondary to this in ensuring a good education for each child.

Instead, lobby for appropriate spending of funds. Minority World countries have immense budgets for schooling as compared to Majority World countries who consistently turn out better schooled students (of those that are able to avail themselves of schooling). There is great mismanagement of funds in the Minority World, and selection of educational priorities is often very poor; for example, millions of dollars are spent on waste removal and disposal, on an endless supply of disposables, wasted hydroelectric energy and wasted paper. Almost all the garbage created in our schools is lunch and snack garbage, and recyclable paper. All this garbage could easily be totally eliminated! With appropriate use of all the other resources enough money would be saved to relieve the shortages of essentials like textbooks, and fine arts programs. It is up to parents and teachers, but only if they have the will to change their priorities, and their lifestyles, and to model the desired behaviours.

SOLUTION #10: MODEL, TEACH, REINFORCE, REWARD AND USE THE TWELVE VALUES OF THE LIVING VALUES EDUCATIONAL PROGRAM.

BECAUSE IT WILL:

~ make everyone more secure,
~ improve communication within the family,
~ create more peace and harmony,
~ develop creativity,
~ lower consumption,
~ improve the environment,
~ reduce global warming,

~ curb climate change,

~ reduce the need for control of global resources through warfare,

~ and **SAVE MONEY.**

HOW IS THAT POSSIBLE?

The L.V.E.P. was developed by the Brahma Kumaris, in conjunction with the U.N. and U.N.E.S.C.O. of Spain, after many years of research to determine twelve values that are universally held, regardless of cultural, religious, spiritual, or economic background. The curriculum developed subsequently is being used to teach children and adults the love for living those twelve values. The sharing of this curriculum is strictly a labour of love, and the resources are offered at a minimal cost. The L.V.E.P. is now used in schools, refugee camps, and other settings in more than eighty-four countries and in over thirty-five languages. This author has no financial interest in L.V.E.P., though is honoured to be on the Canadian advisory board.

The twelve values are: Peace, Respect, Love, Acceptance/Tolerance, Happiness, Humility, Honesty, Responsibility, Cooperation, Freedom, Unity, and Simplicity. Each value is learned, understood and practiced using a diversity of creative activities, which could involve writing, music, dance, drawing, painting, or drama. As a family, or any other group, works through the program, much greater understanding and compassion develop, not only amongst the family members, but also with the larger family of humanity. All the activities develop creative thinking, which in turn teaches how to create more options for problem solving, and more options for decision making on how to live.

Living these values creates a more secure citizenry; thereby reducing materialistic wants, which in turn lead to a cleaner environment and less need for warfare, as previously shown in greater detail. Instead of watching T.V while eating some toxic takeout, why not play together with this program, and make the world a better place for children and for all the rest of Life?

SOLUTION #11; LOBBY YOUR DISTRICT TO PROVIDE STAFF WITH TRAINING IN MEDIA LITERACY, AND THEN FOR PARENTS, STUDENTS AND THE COMMUNITY TO RECEIVE IT FROM THE STAFF

BECAUSE IT WILL:

~ make people feel more secure,
~ free your mind,
~ improve your health,
~ improve the health of the planet,
~ make universal health care more accessible for all,
~ reduce misogyny (therefore homophobia, and help A.I.D.S. victims),
~ reduce the need for warfare, and nuclear weapon amassment,
~ and SAVE MONEY.

HOW IS THAT POSSIBLE?

To be media literate is to discern bias, stereotyping, values, propaganda, half-truths, incomplete information, and have the ability to determine a bigger truth through use of alternative sources for information. The global mainstream mass media (Trash Media) is under the control of a few, all of whom happen to hold similar values to those of the colonizers of five hundred years ago: profit at any cost, every living thing is a commodity, and alternate viewpoints are too dangerous to the bottom line. So, of course, the values being developed in the unthinking public are the only ones being highlighted for them through their Church of the Trash Media, and their worship of trash consumption.

The main goal of the mainstream, privately owned Trash Media is profit; the main goal of publicly owned media is to inform, educate, and entertain through wholesome high quality programming. The same is very true of much of the other socially conscious alternative media.

The Trash Media are responsible only to the advertisers, whose only mandate is to generate profit for the makers of the advertised products and services. Consequently, not only is private media an ongoing barrage of commercials for unnecessary products, but also its emphasis is placed on shallow coverage of local and world affairs. The consumer of this type of media is presented with a very right winged, fundamentalist, capitalist view of the world, full of doom and gloom, with life fulfillment only being possible if one continuously consumes material goods, and non life enhancing services.

Most of the Trash Media advertising is directed at females, in particular young ones. Almost every advertisement seems to be designed to convince females of the inadequacy of every aspect of their being; their hair is not the right color nor is shiny enough, their skin is not glowing, their face is too colourless, their teeth are not white enough; their lips, eyes and breasts are too small; their waist, hips and their thighs are too big; they have too much bodily hair; their mouth, underarms, and genitals smell bad; they need to smoke, drink alcohol, and eat and drink junk to be attractive to a man; they are not trendy enough in their wardrobe; they need to display their wares more; they are simply not acceptable or valuable as they are. This is just another manifestation of misogyny. In becoming media literate females are able to regain control of their self-esteem, and make decisions based on their own needs, not based on the needs of the corporations needing even bigger profits, and the old boys institutions needing to keep women insecure, and thus easier to control.

A disproportionate amount of space is devoted to sports and violence in the mainstream Trash Media, and to a lesser extent, even in the public media. Is there an equivalent amount devoted to the arts and good news? Why not? These things carry inherent feminine values of creativity and compassion, and the primary controllers of Trash Media are misogynistic, giant conglomerates. The media depicts the values of the ones who control the purse strings, and it is of little benefit to them to create a media savvy citizenry.

A media literate person is not easily controlled by advertisers, or by the corporate agenda of the handful of media moguls who own nearly all the media in the world, whether print, audio, visual, electronic, or mixed. As one becomes a more independent thinker one gains control of one's own mind, and takes charge of one's own life, leading to better wellbeing, better decisions, and ultimately to less consumption. It has already been shown how less consumption produces positive results in the global issues of environment, global warming, climate change, warfare, and arms amassment.

SOLUTION # 12: AVAIL YOURSELF OF THE LOCAL LIBRARY MUCH MORE OFTEN THAN THE LOCAL BIG BOX VIDEO STORE
BECAUSE IT WILL:

~ make you and your children smarter,
~ more globally aware,
~ more literate in life skills,
~ more secure and happier,
~ reduce dependency on foreign owned media,
~ develop stronger national sovereignty,
~ reduce violence, crime, and injustices,
~ reduce the desire to buy, buy, buy,
~ and thereby improve the quality of life for all in the biosphere,
~ and **SAVE MONEY**.

HOW IS THAT POSSIBLE?

Education begins at home, and to date, schooling happens in institutions. Making the local library a regular part of the family's life is one of the easiest ways to further everyone's education and make the world a better place for all. Of course, the ideal scenario would be to use the library in conjunction with buying books and other informational resources from local, small businesses. The money spent on the daily specialty coffee would easily buy one good resource per week for the use of the family. Amongst four hundred of the world's recognized eminent people studied it was found that most had been surrounded by books, of substance, in their homes during childhoods. And they had had adults who genuinely modeled a love of life long learning.

Our children do not know what they need to know, and depend upon us to prepare them for adulthood. Many of us adults did not know what we had needed to know in order to have raised educated, good global citizens. We have had access to more information than any previous generation. However, information is not knowledge, and knowledge is not wisdom. Learning from the diversity of library resources is a great start to moving from information, to knowledge, and to wisdom.

Many baby boomer yuppies and their puppies lack the simple life skills needed to implement some of the solutions offered; cooking, sewing, preserving, home management, child rearing, preventative health care, and spiritual practice. Some still have elders to ask for guidance, and virtually all of us have access to libraries and the Internet to learn essential life skills. Having these skills makes one more self sufficient, and a more valuable asset to all of humanity. What use is a Ph.D. or an M.B.A. if our children are dying in record numbers of cancer, diabetes, heart disease, environmental pollution related illnesses, and other preventable causes? What use are able bodied humans who are unable to prepare wholesome sustenance for themselves, or sew on a button, or manage their home? Self-sufficiency needs to be a major goal of effective parenting, and of being human skills.

Still others place their faith in the God of Consumer Goods for an endless supply of cheap quality goods for their bodies, homes, workplaces as well as other parts of their lives. They expect science and technology to find ways to keep them comfortable and to solve all that ails humanity and its only home. There has been very little invented by science and technology in the last century that has been an essential to the life of anything, with the notable exception of the change in perspective on the nature of reality as described by the most advanced quantum physicist-mystics.

It was the case that necessity was the mother of invention, and our ancestors had already cornered the market on basic essentials for survival. We have merely improved on some of these. For the better part of the last century necessity has not been the mother of invention, it has been profit. If most new inventions had come into being because of any genuine human need then today we would not have child poverty (with the USonians having amongst the highest level in the industrialized Minority World), world hunger, homelessness, global warming, nuclear weapons, species extinction, desertification, soil erosion and depletion, and twenty year patents on drugs desperately needed right now by those who can least afford them.

In all fairness there are socially conscious inventors; however, most are not working in military or government sponsored Research And Development, and their inventions hold little leverage in gaining control of world resources, or power over the majority. Without substantial financial backing it is virtually impossible for an altruistic, socially conscious inventor to introduce a product into the mainstream.

The unaware point to medical science and technology to make the point in favour of essential new inventions. Living longer in the industrialized nations is predominantly the result of clean water, better nutrition and hygiene, and minimally due to any medical breakthroughs. This is easily verifiable by looking to areas in poor nations where only water quality, nutrition, and hygiene were improved, producing a dramatic difference in the health, wellbe-ing and longevity of the people. Even if it were true that science and technology of the last century are solely responsible for the longevity of industrialized peoples, could one honestly state that the longevity has been accompanied by a directly proportional increase in the quality of life for all, other than those able to avail themselves financially of limited benefits of new technologies?

Placing faith in science, technology, inventors, and the God of Consumer Goods has neither solved the major global problems, nor improved the quality of life for most. Certainly gadgets have relieved us of some of the drudgery, and borne our burdens at a much faster pace than we could. But, have all the gadgets, appli-ances, and other "stuff" given us the time for life enhancement that we were promised if we bought and used them? The solu-tions do NOT lie in placing more faith in the "universal THEY". The solutions lie within the thoughts, words and deeds of each of us.

Becoming educated leads to a greater sense of psychological se-curity, for true education cultivates all aspects of being human; that is, the emotional, physical, intellectual and spiritual nurture in equal balance. The more secure a person feels, the less is their need to consume material goods or to control others; they are less easily influenced by peers or the Trash Media; they have a stronger locus of internal control; and they are much more likely to pursue altruistic endeavours. It is unlikely that the reader still needs the dots connected by this solution to greater world peace and security for all of Life.

Education entails a life long pursuit of improving ones self in all areas of being human, it does not begin with pre-school and end upon graduation. It begins before birth and continues to the last breath, perhaps even beyond that. Only schooling begins in pre-school and ends with graduation. We have been failing our young for centuries now. We are the only species that fails so miserably, consistently, and blindly.

The following is a parable, by Jon. Rye Kinghorn from A Step-by-Step Guide for Conducting a Consensus and Diversity Workshop in Global Education, illustrating the urgent need to create a society that values and models global citizenship.

> *"Once upon a time there was a class and the students expressed disapproval of their teacher. Why should they be concerned with global interdependence, global problems and what others of the world were thinking, feeling and doing? And the teacher said she had a dream in which she saw one of her students fifty years from today. The student was angry and said, "Why did I learn so much detail about the past and the administration of my country, and so little about the world?" He was angry because no one told him that as an adult he would be faced almost daily with problems of a global interdependent nature, be they problems of peace, security, quality of life, food, inflation, or security of natural resources.*

> *The angry student found he was the victim as well as the beneficiary. "Why was I not warned? Why was I not better educated? Why did my teachers not tell me about the problems and help me understand I was a member of an interdependent human race? "*

> *With even greater anger the student shouted, "You helped me extend my hands with machines, my eyes with telescopes and microscopes, my ears with telephones, radios and sonar, my brain with computers, BUT you did not help me extend my heart, love, concern to the entire human family. You, teacher, gave me only half a loaf."*

Parental priorities of the Western Minded give less than half a loaf to our precious young. How sad that those with the most access to full loaves are least able, or willing, to give them to their children.

These solutions offered in the preceding pages are expected to be extremely unpopular with many Western Minded parents, and with the powers that now control the minds and purse strings of the existing, and those aspiring to be the Western Minded. Nonetheless, the solutions are offered, for one must act fearlessly upon what one believes is right. The solutions above not only provide a full loaf for children, but also they show how to acquire it fairly and peacefully, without placing excessive strains on the natural systems. They will help to raise a much more secure human race, save a lot of money (which, unfortunately, seems to be the bottom line for the Western Minded), and improve the conditions for life for every species of Life.

"You teach us not to fight with others; to work things out; to respect others; to clean up our messes; not to hurt other creatures; to share – not be greedy. Then why do you go out and do the things you tell us not to do? ... What you do makes me cry at night. You grown-ups say you love us. I challenge you, please make your actions reflect your words."

> *Severn Suzuki, at age 12, addressing*
> *the largest gathering of heads of states,*
> *U.N.C.E.D, '72*

CHAPTER NINE:

IN THE MIDDLE

Life of my Life,
I shall ever try to keep my body pure, knowing that thy living touch is upon
all my limbs
I shall ever try to keep all untruths from my thoughts, knowing that thou
are that truth which kindled the light of reason in my mind.
I shall ever try to drive all evils from my heart and keep my love in
flower, knowing that thou hast thy seat in the innermost shrine of my heart.
And it shall be my endeavor to reveal thee in my actions, knowing it is thy
power gives me strength to act.

Robindernath Thakker (which
became "Tagore", after being An-
glicized by the invaders)

This chapter focuses on the day-to-day things we could all do differently, or not do at all, or add to our repertoire of things we do. By now the reader should be becoming more conscious of how the dots connect our actions and choices to very serious global injustices and atrocities. In spite of making the effort to not repeat the links and connections, sometimes it is necessary to restate the obvious. The average person needs to have exposure to something seven or eight times before they, "Get it". So, unless all the readers are gifted, that is, advanced and accelerated in any one or more of the six areas of human ability, the author will proceed as if writing for those of us with average ability. (The gifted "get it " after only one or two exposures.)

None of the solutions offered in this work will appeal to every reader. All that is asked is the reader consider the serious consequences of further inaction. An end to wars, pollution, preventable child deaths, global warming, climate change, genocides, violence against women, enslavement of children in sweatshops, and corporate control of all of Life are within the control of every one of us. We have created all of them and we can end all of them. Do we have the will?

SOLUTION #13: GET RID OF MOST OF THE CABLE CHANNELS, LOOK TO ALTERNATIVE MEDIA FOR MORE AUTHENTIC INFORMATION OF THE WORLD, AND LOOK TO PUBLIC BROADCASTING MORE OFTEN FOR ENTERTAINMENT, EDUCATION AND INFORMATION

BECAUSE IT WILL:

~ help maintain national sovereignty,
~ stop further monoculture-ism,
~ help people become informed, good global citizens,
~ develop understanding, tolerance, and acceptance,
~ break the bonds of global media monopolies,
~ provide more uplifting, diverse entertainment and information,
~ aid in understanding global issues as they affect us and vice versa
~ and SAVE MONEY

HOW IS THAT POSSIBLE?

The single biggest danger to the sovereignty of all nations is the group of Trash Media giants that controls television stations, radio stations, newspapers, magazines and advertising. This group presents a single viewpoint, and not that of most nations. A surprising number of well-schooled North Americans actually believe they are receiving good and thorough news coverage through C.N.N. and other Trash Media. Unfortunately, most of the Trash Media is under the control of a handful of individuals who tend to be of the right wing, fundamentalist, profit-seeking mentality. For them raising awareness of global events is rarely the issue, raising suspicion towards the Others is. Thus, allowing for further neo-colonization without question from the general populace who, on the surface, seem to benefit.

It is due to the revenues earned through advertising that the Trash Media is able to operate, and advertising is only successful if the viewer purchases the goods or services advertised. By switching to higher quality publicly owned media, the viewer is freed from much of the mind control directing us to buy, buy, buy.

Regardless of the country, the global Trash Media creates mono-cultures of unthinking people, content to allow atrocities to continue on their behalf, because the Trash Media has convinced them of the evil intents of others. We, all nations and cultures, need to return to our own forms of entertainment a little more and develop our own cultures. Monoculture in agriculture leads to annihilation of the entire crop in the event of pestilence, drought or other disaster. This also would be the case with monoculture of the human race once options are reduced to one way of being.

The Western Minded have much easier access to alternative media, and yet most do not choose to avail themselves of it. They spend countless hours with trashy women's magazines, sports news, selecting coffee, buying products for their hair, and blaming the whole world for their minor inconveniences of slow online services. Turn off the colonization of the mind and learn about the world we share from many sources, so that we can be more effective citizens in this totally interdependent world. Once we understand the issues more fully we can act on them. That is the last thing desired by those who control the Trash Media, for often they are also the governments, multi-national corporations and international financial institutions, that perpetuate the local and global issues.

The choice is ours; to remain ignorant and controlled, or to taste of the forbidden fruit of a bigger truth and develop the kind of world we really want to see for ourselves and for our children in which to grow?

SOLUTION #14: ESTABLISH A REGULAR SPIRITUAL PRACTICE

BECAUSE IT WILL:

~ help create world peace,
~ improve health and wellbeing,
~ make universal health care accessible to all,
~ stop cultural colonization by multinational and transnational corporations,
~ improve the health of the planetary biosphere,
~ reduce the desire for material goods,
~ reduce arms amassment and wars,
~ and **SAVE MONEY**.

HOW IS THAT POSSIBLE?

It is unfortunate that spirituality and religion do not refer to the same thing in reality. The former predates the latter by many, many centuries, and does not require membership into a group with a mediator between humans and the Divine. There are very strong spiritual traditions at the heart of every religion, the mystical origins, mostly unpracticed by the followers. The current list of nearly all major traditions, established within the last 3500 years or so, were all created by men, for men, about men, and have no place for women as humans of intrinsic value. They all teach the reverence of womanhood only because women have the wombs that carried the founders of the faiths, the saints and leaders. This is as ludicrous as teaching respect for men only because they produce sperm in their testicles which might sire kings!

In effect, organized religions tend to exclude the inherent value of the feminine and female, and thus disqualifying themselves from being vehicles for spiritual development, in this author's view.

Spirituality entails taking personal responsibility for evolving into the best human being one can be, not out of fear of some external father figure, or out of desire for some imaginary afterlife. But out of the sheer joy of making and maintaining connection with the source of one's being, without intermediaries. This could be done within a religious tradition, if the hierarchy permits it. At the very least it involves meditation, prayer, gratitude, and creativity. A mountain of research has shown that people who meditate and, or pray are calmer, healthier, and more content; that group meditation and prayer are even more powerful; and even A.D.H.D. children practicing meditation regularly, along with a whole foods diet, can eliminate allopathic drugs for the most part.

Spiritual practices can take many forms, and if genuine and authentic, they will not interfere with any religions. In fact, they will enhance one's religious life. The simple act of breathing deeply and mindfully can be one such simple practice; others include various forms of meditation, prayer, solitude, liturgical dance or music, appreciation of the natural world, contemplation of any of the world's inspirational works, creating beauty, doing service, and genuinely loving a child. "Genuine loving" means having the ACTIVE will to nurture the wellbeing of another.

A regular spiritual practice improves health, wellbeing, and the desire to avoid or create social/emotional, intellectual and physical toxins'; namely entertainment based on violence, apathy towards the less privileged, non-nutritious foods and neglect of the natural environment. With less need for the Trash Media, and more awareness of the planetary consequences of one's actions one further reduces the power of multinational media moguls to colonize minds, and that further reduces the desire to accumulate stuff. "Stuff" is almost always a petroleum product, or needs the energy of fossil fuels for manufacture, and is made by minors in Majority World sweatshops.

PEACE IS NOT ONLY ABOUT AN ABSENCE OF WAR!

It is about personal security as one goes about one's life. Women do not have it any where in the world, most of the Majority World does not have it, the Indigenous do not have it, the differently gendered do not have it, the millions of homeless in the industrialized Minority World do not have it, and certainly no living species in the polluted biosphere has it. By becoming more peaceful ourselves we will do more to facilitate the development of peace for all, than a thousand protests, or finger pointing at the "universal They". "Let there be peace and let it begin with the way I choose to live", Grade 7 class's Remembrance Day project, 2004. This requires a daily time commitment, just as do making real food for one's family or teaching life skills to one's children. If we are unable to make time for these things then what good are we as a species? Unless, of course, being an H.I.V./A.I.D.S. like virus in the biosphere is what we consider being of good use as a species.

Spiritual bankruptcy is at the root of almost all that plagues humanity today. No problems of the world have been the result of any spiritual practice; many have been and continue to be the result of religious practices. In fact, people wishing to develop their spiritual nature are being persecuted in China, Tibet, and in Western nations where fundamentalist governments have control.

How simple: develop one's spirituality and make the world a better place for all of Life.

SOLUTION #15: ELIMINATE CONSUMPTION OF DISPOSABLES

BECAUSE IT WILL:

~ clean up environmental pollutants,
~ improve the health of our families,
~ lower health care costs,
~ make universal health care a reality,
~ slow down depletion of all natural resources,
~ lower the rates of cancer in our children,
~ relieve child labour,
~ thwart nuclear weapon amassments,
~ promote greater justice for all,
~ and **SAVE MONEY.**

HOW IS THAT POSSIBLE?

It is very inconvenient to use permanent, and long-term use items, such as real plates, mugs, cutlery, cloth dishrags and towels, lunch bags and containers, … One has to pay more initially, wash them, try not to lose them, get one's hands wet and dirty, have enough space to store them, … We must ask ourselves how inconvenient is it for the children undergoing chemotherapy, or the children working in sweat shops, or the creatures becoming extinct as a result of one time use disposables? It is the Western Minded that cause all this to happen with their demands for the convenience of everything throw away?

Almost every item purchased by the Western Minded is a disposable; that is, it is thrown away once it has outlived its one time convenient use (which one might add has become true of relationships too). Cutlery, crockery, napkins, paper towels, straws, shopping bags, food wrappers, gift wraps, containers for toiletries, cosmetics, cleansers, auto needs, yard needs, electronics, razors, drink boxes, cheap quality synthetic clothing and footwear, accessories, table linens, cameras, and the list goes on, and on, and on. Perfectly good natural resources, mostly wood and petroleum, are removed from the Earth involving environmentally dangerous and hazardous processes, and converted into items for throwing away. Huge industries have been built for this and have a highly vested financial interest in maintaining this genocidal habit.

Briefly, the links are: use of petroleum fuels wars and weapons amassment, depletion of trees for wood increases green house gasses and increases desertification, soil depletion; use of other chemicals for manufacture creates environmental pollution, the two latter create more illnesses, more indentured minors in Majority World sweat-shops who produce many of the disposables; all synthetic items off gas and add to the carcinogen build up in children... Need one continue?

The Western Minded throw away an average of twelve disposables a day; coffee cups, paper towels, food wraps, drink containers, packaging of various sorts, coasters, straws... Daily that is roughly, 20% times 6.4 billion times 12, or 15.6 billion items thrown away. Few of these are reclaimable to begin with, and the few that are reclaimable are rarely reclaimed. If one adds to this all that is thrown away which is reclaimable (paper, glass, aluminum, cardboard, natural fibers, organic waste) the numbers become mind numbing. All this waste turns into toxic sludge, acid rain, and pollutants in the land, sea, and air, at home and abroad.

Oh yes, we are now making food containers out of corn and some other crops that will biodegrade. How stupid and thoughtless! Growing the crops requires fertilizers, pesticides, insecticides, water, machinery, valuable land, fossil fuels and hydroelectric energy. Manufacture of these crops into packaging requires fossil fuels. Shipping and disposal require fossil fuels. Also, we import these crops from Majority World countries, so the poor continue to starve, and we continue to throw away their lives.

Every moment of every day a beautiful, vibrant, life-sustaining body is having tiny portions removed from it continuously, only to be replaced by previously unknown, and unnatural parts that inhibit the growth of life in this body. At some critical point in the near future this body will cease to be live, or be able to support any life. This is what we do to the living biosphere every moment of every day as we convert all that is healthy and natural into millions of mountains of un-biodegradable trash, which nurtures the growth of nothing natural, and kills thousands of innocent children weekly.

Do we really need to carry a drink with us everywhere? Can we not last a couple of hours without a drink in a disposable cup, box, can or bottle? Do we really need to buy coffee from some foreign owned company that acquires its coffee from unfairly paid farmers, using dangerous chemicals and unsafe farming practices, while being unethical in its dealings with its employees in retail outlets, and be unpaid advertising for it by carrying its name brand paper and plastic mugs? Do we have the will to get organized and have a decent breakfast with our families so that the early morning drive-through and pick-up facilities become obsolete? How did our mothers and fathers manage without name brand coffee cups, plastic shopping bags, and all the other things we throw away daily?

There are an estimated 30,000,000 known species currently. There is only one amongst these that devotes enormous resources, enormous human power, and enormous quantities of time to making things for the sole purpose of throwing them away. It is the only species that knowingly poisons its young. It is the only species that has created nuclear weapons to destroy every living thing on the surface of the Earth. It is the only species that has driven thousands of species into extinction. It is the only species that has polluted every body of water, land and pockets of air we breathe. It is the only species that has made it impossible for its young to just be in the radiance of our Sun without risk of cancer. It is the only species that claims to be the one species having a rational intelligence!!!!!!!

CHART #5: ON DISPOSABLES AND SINGLE USE ITEMS

PRIMARILY DISPOSABLES ARE MADE OF WOOD PRODUCTS OR PETROLEUM PRODUCTS. SINGLE USE ITEMS MADE OF GLASS OR METAL ARE NOT DISCUSSED HERE, BECAUSE IT IS HOPED THAT THESE ARE BEING RECYCLED INSTEAD OF BEING DISCARDED. STILL OTHERS ARE MADE OF COMBINATIONS OF MATERIALS, SUCH AS TETRAPACKS. THE FOLLOWING ONLY DEALS WITH WOOD BASED DISPOSABLE ITEMS. BY NOW THE READER SHOULD BE ABLE TO EXTRAPOLATE FOR PETROLEUM BASED DISPOSABLES; THAT IS, ALL THE PLASTICS AND COMBINATION DISPOSABLE PRODUCTS. WOOD BASED DISPOSABLES REQUIRE CERTAIN RESOURCES, AS SHOWN BELOW, WHICH NEED OTHERS, AND CUMULATIVELY HAVE THE LISTED EFFECTS.

TREES

a) **trees from monoculture farming** ◊ reduce essential biodiversity, increase species extinction, deplete soil nutrients, increase siltation of waters, decrease air cleaning capacity, increase greenhouse gasses, speed up global warming, extreme effects of climate increase, more environmental refugees, loss of property, greater incidence of cancer and other environment related illnesses.

b) **trees from old growth** ◊ diminish sensitive habitat, decrease lung capacity of Earth, and all of the above

c) **trees from temperate, tropical, mangrove or cloud rain forests** ◊ loss of biodiversity forever, soil becomes useless after a few years, increase desertification, force relocation of, and cultural genocide of rain forest dwellers, and all of the above.

OTHER NATURAL RESOURCES

a) **petroleum** for plastic coating, tetra-packs etc ◊ see Chart #3 page 88.

b) **crops** for biodegradable disposables with wood products◊see Chart #1 page 76.

ALSO NEEDED ARE FACTORIES, RETAIL OUTLETS, TRANSPORTATION, PACKAGING, ADVERTISING, WASTE DISPOSAL. See Chart #3 for the impact and consequences.

IN SUMMARY:

1 Nearly every step of every process in making, and dealing with the waste created does the following:
   ~ deplete limited natural resources
   ~ use fossil and hydroelectric fuels
   ~ increase environmental damage to land, sea and air
   ~ deplete protective layer in the biosphere
   ~ increase greenhouse gasses, global warming and climate change
   ~ decrease essential biodiversity
   ~ decrease capacity of the biosphere to self regulate

2 Many of the disposables, or portions thereof, are made in Majority World sweatshops by minors who have no protection with labour laws or environmental regulations.

3 Some of the most significant consequences include
   ~ there is an increase in warfare over control of limited resources
   ~ this gives rise to an increase in arms amassment, including nuclear, chemical and biological
   ~ millions of humans are adversely effected by environment related illnesses, such as cancer
   ~ universal health care is becoming less of a reality for more and more people due to the overuse of the medical system dealing with self inflicted illnesses. This is giving greater impetus to right wing governments to privatize health care out of affordability for most.
   ~ the numbers of environmental refugees are rising, in particular in areas of great poverty
   ~ there is more frequent extreme and unpredictable weather, causing loss of life, property, and species.
   ~ millions in the Majority World suffer human rights abuse, environment related ill health with little or no access to medical care due to structural adjustment programs, and their lands are being used as dumping ground for our disposable items. Thus, further increasing serious health and wellbeing issues for them.

ONE MAY SUBSTITUTE ANY OTHER DISPOSABLE ITEM FOR THE ABOVE AND FIND THAT THE DAMAGE DONE BY THE ROUTINE USE OF THESE IS SO IMMENSE THAT CONTINUED USE IS NOTHING SHORT OF DELIBERATE GENOCIDE OF THE ENTIRE HUMAN RACE, AND MANY OTHER INNOCENT SPECIES.

SOLUTION #16: INGEST MUCH LESS ANIMAL PROTEIN

BECAUSE IT WILL:

~ improve the health of all of Life,
~ lower medical costs,
~ make universal health care a reality for all,
~ reduce Majority World poverty and hunger,
~ reduce environmental pollutants,
~ curb global warming and climate change,
~ reduce wars and arms amassment,
~ reduce the monopolies of agri-businesses,
~ help people become more compassionate,
~ and **SAVE MONEY.**

HOW IS THAT POSSIBLE?

It is a myth of the meat and dairy industries that humans must consume non-human animal proteins or perish. Most of the world is, and always has been predominantly vegetarian, with the occasional use of non-human animal protein as a condiment. Massive dinosaurs of the past, huge animals of today, and many world-class athletes are, or have been vegetarians. Even in ancient and prehistoric times the young, the elderly and the infirmed thrived on plant based diets provided by the women during the extended absences of men, away in search of meat. Being a strict vegetarian is not being promoted here. What is being asked is that the Western Minded dramatically reduce their consumption of meat and dairy in order for others to just live.

Unlike the past when livestock roamed freely, ate toxin free feed free of same species remains, and was slaughtered humanely, today factory farms produce meat from stressed livestock. There is nothing humane in this method. Large numbers of animals are kept in very cramped conditions, filled with chemicals for rapid growth, and butchered in great pain. The feed required for these animals occupies roughly twelve times the acreage needed to grow the same poundage of grains or cereals for human consumption. The amount of water needed for every pound of meat is nearly a hundred times what is needed to produce the same amount of crops for human consumption. The amount of caloric energy input needed to get a pound of meat is more than twelve times more than what is retrieved by the human body from a pound of meat. Much of the feed is exported from Majority World farms, where the levels of hunger and poverty are heart breaking.

Imagine repeatedly investing a million dollars in the stock market knowing only a thousand will be recuperated. Too silly for an intelligent species to waste time imagining: but, not to silly for the Western Minded of the species to do repeatedly with respect to its animal protein intake!

Methane, one of the greenhouse gasses, is produced when organic matter decomposes in the absence of oxygen; such as in rice paddies and the intestines of cows. The factory farming of millions of heads of cattle produces a very significant amount of methane, adding to global warming, climate change and all the disasters that accompany these. A large bulk of the beef produced is for the fast food industry, where the food has virtually no nutritional value, all the while doing much harm to human health and to the environment by the industry. Old growth and rainforests in South America were cleared to graze scrawny cattle on rich soil, which soon became devoid of nutrients following a couple of years of use for grazing. The displaced aboriginal peoples of the rainforests now have all the social problems of most aboriginal cultures contacted by the Western Minded greed.

Simply put, the amount of land, crops, water and energy input required to produce a pound of meat exceed many, many times what is gained. The harmful chemicals fed the livestock, as well as the harmful chemicals used to grow the feed given the livestock, find their way into human bodies. They also find their way into the communal ground water when the animals eliminate their waste. Meat consumption is directly linked to many health issues, in young and old. What used to be the diseases of the kings are now the diseases of the common, for now they too daily dine like kings on a heavy diet of non-human animal protein. The ground under hard hoofed animals becomes too hard packed, unable to breathe, to be of much use for growing anything, as has happened in Australia.

The damage done by the packaging, shipping and discarding of packaging for the meat industry has already been discussed. All the farm machinery and chemicals used need petroleum, the control of which is the chief reason for current occupations and wars. Use of petroleum and other fossil fuels in the production of meat creates environmental pollutants, furthers global warming and climate change. Also required is a good deal of electrical energy, which is derived from dammed waterways, causing further environmental damage to the land, many species, and unsuccessful relocation of humans.

There is enough food grown to feed the entire world. It is the unjust sharing of it that starves the majority in order to feed the livestock of the minority. We deprive the Majority World poor even further by forcing export crop production to feed Minority World livestock. The poor nation's farmers DO NOT get enough revenue to buy food for survival, and they cannot grow food for themselves.

The dairy industry does similar damage, and is equally inhumane. We are the only species that continues to drink milk after being weaned, and are the only species that drinks the milk of other species. There are many other sources of calcium, protein and other nutrients found in milk and milk products, and they have more health benefits for humans and the planet than dairy products.

It is not necessary to completely eliminate meat and dairy; however, reducing consumption will improve the quality of life for everything on Earth. Going even further, and only consuming organic, range fed will help restore the nutrients in the severely depleted soils, and produce more nutritious foods. A much lesser quantity of food is needed when consuming nutrient rich organic foods.

For those who adhere to the spiritual belief of ahimsa, no harm to any of Life, or would wish to further their spiritual growth, becoming vegetarian is an excellent place to start. Being vegetarian does not mean living only on fruits and vegetables. There are numerous sources to find direction in that area. There are the ridiculous few who argue on behalf of vegetables to not be eaten either. That is well and good if one is willing to end one's life by consuming nothing out of respect for, or fear of harming another life. However, since most of us are not willing to end our lives consciously, the advice being given is to eat low on the food chain, eat fresh, eat local, and eat seasonal. Most of the Western Minded people are ending their lives earlier unconsciously with their lifestyle of extreme laziness.

If these global costs are not sufficient reasons to make the change, then keep in mind the personal cost savings of buying less non-human animal protein, and the personal cost of savings due to better health. Too often the latter is the only argument that appeals to the comfortable Western Minded.

SOLUTION #17: BUY LOCAL, UNION MADE GOODS, AND DO NOT SUPPORT THE FOREIGN OWNED BIG BOX STORE CHAINS (The Big B.S.) BECAUSE IT WILL:

~ provide employment locally with fair wages,
~ protect national sovereignty,
~ diminish human rights violations,
~ improve the environment,
~ reduce global warming and climate change,

~ help eliminate the reasons for foreign occupations and warfare,
~ decrease the monopolies of multinational corporations,
~ reduce poverty, hunger and homelessness,
~ and **SAVE MONEY** in the long run.

HOW IS THAT POSSIBLE?

The foreign owned big box stores (The Big B.S.) can supply goods at a cheaper price than nationally or locally owned businesses are able to do. But, the actual price is too great to even measure accurately. Almost all the goods in the Big B.S., like Sprawl Marts, Home Despots, Painmore Shoes, Starvebucks are made in the sweatshops of the Majority World. The links to this and human rights, environment, monopolies, and peace have already been addressed. Even if the goods are a designer brand they are cheaply made and need to be replaced far sooner than better quality, local, union made goods. Thus, costing more money to replace more often, causing more misery for the foreign child workers, creating more ill health through environmental pollution, and requiring more resources, including fuel for international import and export item transportation.

Purchase of locally made goods boosts the national economy, furthers the goals of national self-sufficiency and sovereignty, and provides a living wage for families. It has been well documented that the laborers, mostly very young girls, in sweatshops do not receive a living wage, they are abused, work in hazardous conditions with no labour standards or environmental regulations. It is not only foreign workers who suffer, but also the local retail outlet employees of the Big B.S.; they rarely have job security, benefits, or enough work hours to support their families. The vast majority are women who have had few opportunities to further their education, or to obtain full time employment elsewhere. They are threatened, intimidated, bullied, and harassed, if not fired, if they attempt to organize for living wages and job security. Or, the employers simply pack up and leave if the law of the land seems to be in support of the workers, and take with them the millions of dollars of profits already gleaned from the blood, sweat and tears of foreign and local labourers.

Paying a little more for better quality generally leads one to treat items with a little more care and respect, the items last longer, require fewer replacements, and therefore lessening the burden to the environment and reducing what fuels the need to control global resources, and amass weapons of mass destruction.

There are few of the Western Mindset who have a pressing financial need to purchase goods from the Big B.S.. They do seem to have a pressing need to have their hearts tested for callousness and their heads tested for hypocrisy. There are many pressing needs of the rest of Life that go unmet by promoting the Big B.S.. There are too many good reasons to boycott such stores and work for global justice, and only one, very selfish one, to continue to patronize them; the complete thoughtlessness and laziness of the Western Minded, who seem to know only price, but not cost.

Every time we purchase an item, or place another item in the garbage bin we need to ask; at what cost did I enjoy this convenience? How many did I harm with my laziness? What could I do differently in the future so that I do not have this thing that needs to be thrown away? Is my laziness, and the harm it does to all of Life, consistent with what my religion tells me about being my sibling's keeper?

Every moment we give over to the Trash Media is a moment that could have enhanced the quality of our lives, and thus enhancing the quality of life for all of Life. This is the case for implementing every other solution presented. Are we willing to make our actions match our words of concern for the state of the world?

CHAPTER TEN:

AROUND THE HOME

Save us
From our folly, by your wisdom
From our arrogance, by your forgiving love,
From our greed, by your infinite bounty,
And from our insecurity, by your healing power.
                                    Muslim Prayer

The Western Minded live in relative comfort, and are the ones with the most options and choices. Unfortunately, most of our choices are based on convenience, not on communion with all of Life. Following are a few suggested solutions for bringing communion with Life into our daily actions. Offered are suggestions on yard, garden, vehicle, body and other household products. We may be mentally sick of house and yard work, but it does not have to make us physically sick. Our house and yard work really are killing us, and every other living thing on this planet.

SOLUTION #18: USE ONLY BIODEGRABLE, CRUELTY FREE, MINIMALLY PACKAGED CLEANSERS, YARD, GARDEN AND CAR CARE PRODUCTS
BECAUSE IT WILL:

~ improve the health of all living things, including the biosphere,
~ loosen the mind hold of advertisers,
~ reduce our dependence on petroleum,
~ reduce the reasons for wars over control of oil,
~ reduce global warming,
~ reduce rate of climate change,
~ reduce illness and the use of the medical system,
~ make universal health care more accessible to all,
~ reduce the numbers working in sweat shops around the world,
~ improve the health of the environment,
~ reduce the risk of creating more environmental refugees worldwide,
~ and **SAVE MONEY**.

HOW IS THAT POSSIBLE?

The Apostles of Advertising would have us believe that every one lives in total filth and disgusting conditions, and that the advertised cleansers are desperately needed to clean this filth. If the home of the average, comfortable, Western Minded person is as grossly filthy and stained as the ads show, then that person deserves to live in that filth. Barring extreme circumstances, Western Minded people keep their homes fairly clean and tidy. The extreme products advertised used for daily cleaning are unnecessary for cleaning most households. Almost every part of a home can be cleaned with various combinations of water, baking soda, Borax, vinegar, ammonia, olive oil, citrus juice, peroxide, and elbow grease. There are a few horror stories related to the products made of these ingredients; however, they make up a very tiny percentage of the total number of horror stories related to the toxic chemical cleansers. The toxic cleanser stories are rarely told, for that would not be in the financial interest of the Trash Media that is being sponsored by the chemical company conglomerates. The manufacture of the chemical cleaners alone spews out at least as many pollutants as the use of them spews into our homes, drains and yards.

The toxic cleansers fill your home with gasses, liquids and solids that permeate living organisms, and add to the build up of carcinogens. All the toxins poured down the drains during cleaning eventually find their way into the communal ground water. Paper towels are the preferred weapons of mass destruction of the lazy, who seem to feel they are above getting their hands wet and dirty in cleaning up their own messes. The removal of trees, the manufacture of the towels and their disposal, create very large amounts of environmental damage, deplete limited resources, and give impetus to rogue states to inflict war on other nations over control of the resources. These add more to the burden on the environment that is created with toxic cleansers, which then adversely effects every child on the Earth. Once again, all the chemical cleansers need petroleum byproducts, and the link of that to wars over resources should be well ingrained in the reader by this point.

Very similar reasoning applies to the toxic chemicals for the yard, garden, and car care products. They all find their way into communal ground water, and the air we all breath.

A great many of the products and packages are manufactured in the Majority World under few, if any, environmental or labour standards. Other than damage done to humans with abuses of their rights, the damage done to the environment "over there" does not just stay over there. All this happens in one living system, our biosphere.

Millions of non-human animals are mutilated, maimed, and murdered during testing of products for humans. This alone is reason enough to buy cruelty free products. Some would argue that many of these innocent creatures are specifically bred for this purpose, as if that in it self is not immoral. If humans need these products so desperately, then test them on humans first. We DO NOT NEED most of these products. The corporations advertising these products need our money, to control more of the world.

Using fewer and planet friendly products improves the quality of life for the entire biosphere and all who inhabit it. You may be sick of looking after your house, yard and vehicles. Rest assured, looking after them has been very diligent in making you sick, for a long time now, while killing our children with cancer.

The quality of a person's character is not measured by how white their whites are, or how weed free and manicured their yard is, or how shiny their car is. It is measured by the degree to which they are willing to actively live their espoused beliefs about fairness, justice, world peace, and compassion for all of Life.

SOLUTION #19: USE ONLY BIODEGRADABLE, CRUELTY FREE TOILETRIES AND COSMETICS
BECAUSE AND HOW:

For all the same reasons as have been given for Solution #15.

Additionally, everything applied to the skin, nails, hair, and teeth is absorbed into the body and if it contains toxins they are added to the buildup of cancer producing toxins. The manufacture of the products, the packaging, and the containers, and then the disposal of the packaging and containers add further pollutants. The manufacture, packaging, and disposal, all require fossil fuels.

A different choice would make everyone healthier, create peace and security, and save a lot of money.

Are these not enough reasons to stop using unnecessary products, and to use only a limited amount of cruelty free ones? If a certain hair gel, or a certain toothpaste is going to make you into a more desirable person, then there should be no lonely singles, or unhappy people left in any of the nations of the Western Minded.

SOLUTION #20: RETROFIT YOUR HOME TO MAKE IT MORE ENERGY EFFICIENT, AND KEEP VEHICLES WELL TUNED
BECAUSE IT WILL:
~ improve the environment,
~ make your family healthier,
~ make universal health care a reality for all,
~ slowdown global warming and climate change,
~ reduce the need for wars over resources,
~ reduce the need for amassment of W.M.D.,
~ reduce species extinction,
~ promote national sovereignty,
~ and **SAVE MONEY** in the long run.

HOW IS THAT POSSIBLE?

Most of the "Because it will…" should now be evident to the reader. The sovereignty issue becomes clear when one realizes self-sufficiency in a nation is a far superiour weapon to arms in protecting ones sovereignty. In using less energy and fewer natural resources we improve the health of everything in the biosphere, and we also reduce our dependency on others to provide it for us.

Self-sufficiency was one of the pillars of Gandhi ji's teachings, and using this principle he freed a nation of half a billion from the greedy and cruel clutches of a well armed invader. The same principle can free brain washed people from the clutches of the God of Consumer Goods and his Apostles of Advertising. This can only happen if people feel secure in who they are, and thus become less susceptible to mental or emotional manipulations forcing them to perform the dances choreographed by the God of Consumer Goods and his Apostles.

REDUCE, REDUCE, REDUCE, consumption of all non-essentials, especially petroleum based synthetics and disposables! This is the single most effective solution to most of the big issues. If it is really important to our friends and guests that we have this, that and the other thing, then perhaps we should look elsewhere for friendships. And if, instead, it is really important to us to protect our biosphere, then we need to extricate ourselves from our complicity in harming all of Life.

CHAPTER 11:
BY GENDER

Wake up Woman!
The cock is crowing;
It's three a.m.
Wake up — its time to weed the fields
 in the distant hills.
Sleep no more;
Arise from the burdens of yesterday,
Forget the hours of toil
In the hot sun
That arose when you worked in the field
But set while you hurried to clear the weeds.
In the dark you return, as you left,
To those cooking pots.
Alas! The day is over
When the family enjoys the day's meal
But before you rest your feet
A voice calls: Woman get me hot water!
With that you know it's over
Until the cock crows
And the cycle begins again:
Wake up Woman!
Wake up Woman!

   Arise To The Day's Toil, Assumpta Acam Oturu, Uganda

The term "gender" is preferable to the use of "sex", for it allows for all the ambiguities of human sexuality, and offers more valid options to every individual. Ten percent of humanity is strictly heterosexual, ten percent is strictly homosexual, and the other eighty percent is somewhere in between, ranging from one same sex encounter to full bi-sexuality. In defining belonging to a group with respect to sexual organs, the term "sex" indicates the nature of ones genitalia, and even then there are many who are differently "sexed" than the two dominant forms, and thus they too are excluded from belonging. On the other hand "gender" allows for self-identification based on all four intertwined parts of being human, since gender encompasses much more than ones physical bodily parts.

This chapter offers some advice to the female and male genders and sexes. There are many with female genitalia who posses more maleness than femaleness, and vice versa. This does tend to create a little confusion when trying to write for the one or the other. So, the author leaves it to the reader to determine which part is best suited to them. However, the hope is that all genders will read, and take to heart, all the parts.

PART ONE: FOR FEMALES

To address the entire range of human gendered-ness is not the aim of this work. So, to keep it simple, for the time being, the term "women" will be used in this work to refer to those that have been placed in the traditional roles of females, and generally are females by sex.

It has been determined that females make up 52%of the global population, that they are genetically superiour to males with re-spect to biological survival mechanisms, that 42% of all house-holds are headed by single women, and that women do more than two-thirds of all the work that is done by humans, whether as soldiers, bankers, mothers, farmers, writers, sweepers, or as house spouses. However, women earn only one-tenth of all the money that is earned world wide, and own one one-hundredth of all the property that is owned. If a North American stay-at-home-mother were to be paid for all she does she would receive an annual salary upwards of $110,000.00 U.S.. On the other hand, of all the money that is spent on purchasing consumer goods, it is women that spend over eighty percent of it, mostly on their families and households.

THIS OFFERS WOMEN EIGHTY PERCENT OF THE WORLD'S SPENDING POWER TO CHANGE THE WORLD WITH ONE SIMPLE TOOL.

The God of Consumer Goods is fully aware of this and that is precisely why nearly all his Advertising Apostles aim for female wallets. They have been very insidious in brain washing women into believing in the need for thousands of products that do absolutely nothing useful, or extra-ordinary in reality. For example, just a little research will prove to you that the best beauty secrets for your skin, hair, eyes, teeth, slender waistline, and youthful longevity are found in your diet and life style. You DO NOT NEED all the lotions, potions, and new and improved mixtures and concoctions to have glowing skin, shiny and strong nails and teeth, bright eyes, and enjoy the energy of your youth. Perhaps we do need just a little help, but overall a diet of whole foods, pure water, gentle to moderate exercise, and a spiritual practice will give you everything the jars, bottles, pots, packets, injections, surgery, and personal trainers promise at a high price, and only deliver temporarily. This is a guarantee! Following this advice will make the world a better place for all of Life, and save each of us thousands of dollars yearly. This will release money which could be used for fighting for the rights of those who can not fight themselves.

We, the Western Minded, are very fortunate to be so enlightened that we do not need to subject our females to ritual burnings as they do in India, or honour killings as they do in the Arab world, or clitorodectomies as they do in some parts of Africa, or be sold into the sex trade as they do in South East Asia, or other barbaric customs to which women are subjected in so many parts of the world. Oh no, we are too enlightened for any of those! Instead, we so pressure the females of the Western Minded world to loathe every aspect of their being that they will willingly commit atrocities directly upon themselves. Atrocities such a bulimia, anorexia, cosmetic surgery, cancer promoting tanning beds, painful waxing, shaving, plucking, application of known carcinogens in cosmetic and toiletries, and even accept domestic and sexual abuse as their own fault. Yes, we the Western Minded are too enlightened to harm our females with publicly denounced rituals. And, feeling that we have now corrected injustices towards our females we are now compelled to point fingers at the barbaric treatment of women elsewhere, and demand that the "universal They" do something about it to help.

Women **everywhere** need help, and the best help is to ensure educational opportunities for women and girls. When a female is educated it improves the quality of life for the entire family, improving the economy, and the health and wellbeing of the entire group, be it a tribe or nation. We, the Western Minded, have the highest levels of schooling and yet our females are amongst the least educated; they are unable to think for themselves, being controlled by the Trash Media, and are quite out of balance with respect to the four integrated parts of being human. Furthermore, because of their buying power our females have become the unwitting slave owners worldwide, exploiters and destroyers of the biosphere, and the reason for wars over control of the Earth's resources.

The Western Minded female is brainwashed from birth into believing that she is of little value as she is, and that in order to be acceptable she must aspire to all values traditionally considered masculine, as well as modifying every part of her body in order to attract and keep a male. The first two assertions have been addressed in the schooling and education section. The truth of the latter is apparent in the cacophonous din of product advertising for every square micrometer of the female body, external and internal. Is there anything about being female that has not become something to be fixed using some product or service?

The God of Consumer Goods and his Advertising Apostles have also convinced women to buy pre-packaged toxic foods, toxic drinks (sports drinks, drink crystals, flavoured cocktails, soft drinks, chocolate mixes….), toxic cleansers, reams of synthetic trendy clothes, mindless women's magazines, trashy novels, mountains of disposables, and many, many items for protection from the Sun, the air, the water, and the very land that gives you sustenance. How absurd that we should purchase garments, made of petroleum products, to protect our children from U.V. rays that are now harmful as a result of overuse and abuse of all fossil fuels? How can we continue to not see the tragic irony of this?

Water needs to become pure again and not more bottled water; the soil needs replenishing to grow nutrition loaded plants again and not stronger vitamins and supplements; the air needs to be breathable not more efficient air-quality health alerts; human pores need to excrete waste not be clogged with antiperspirants; natural fragrances need to fill the Earth again, not air fresheners and candles that off-gas toxic substances; and human life needs to be maintained at optimum health through proactive holistic means, not "cut and pasted" solely through reactive allopathic means in response to self-inflicted dis-eases.

"STOP MAKING MORE EFFICIENT WHAT OUGHT NOT BE DONE IN THE FIRST PLACE!"

Anonymous (who was probably a woman, and could only get her voice heard under this pseudonym)

Sisters, the institutions were changing slowly till the neo-conservative force came out to halt any further progress for women, minorities, and the biosphere. In order to save our children from all the horrors of global warming, A.I.D.S., nuclear weapons, enslavement to branding and addiction to selfish convenience, we can dramatically expedite the change. With every penny we spend we can start to see the positive results of our choices, right before our very eyes. By changing the consumption habits of our families we become the change agents creating world peace, a healthy biosphere, and justice for all species.

If you love your family use your purchasing power to show love for them, not to show love for your own laziness and convenience.

PART TWO: FOR MALES

There was a time when the roles for the sexes were more clearly delineated. Women, out of biological imperative, took care of babies, staying closer to home, and therefore becoming the caregivers for the elderly and the infirmed too. The women could not wait several days for the men to return with meat, and so, became adept at providing sustenance and medical care from whatever grew nearby. They became genetically hardwired for multi-tasking and protecting that bit of homeland that sustained and cared for their families and communities. Men became more adept at single focus tasks, such as hunting for dinner at substantial distances from home, or becoming dinner if distracted by multi-tasking. Current brain function research confirms the nature of the differences in hard wiring of males and females, which evolved for the survival of the species.

These are just facts, neither good nor bad in themselves. However, the ability of females to use more parts of their brains, combined with the extra-ordinary efforts made to convert our girls into boys (see the section on schooling and education), have now resulted in a gross unfairness towards our boys and men. Girls are outstripping boys in nearly every academic discipline, creating feelings of inadequacy and insecurity in the boys, whom the media and society advise must be smarter than girls. The Trash Media portrays males variously as wealthy and powerful, or as totally incompetent buffoons, or as violently base creatures. The first implication being that to be a real man, a boy must be smarter, richer and more powerful than females, and other men. Since the only measures for success the Western Minded have are grades and money, boys left far behind in school feel unsuccessful. Then as adult males they are once again left behind, because, many females no longer need the economic security a man's money once provided, and so they continue to feel unsuccessful and inadequate. Secondly, the sit-com and advertising industry's portrayal of men as incompetent buffoons being outshined by more savvy females does little to improve the feelings of insecurity and inadequacy in our boys and men. The third consequence is that even more creative ways of violating women are shown to the already deranged, and insecure. Unfortunately, all these lead to more acts of misogyny.

Some would argue that violence portrayed in the media has no effect on the viewers. If this is true, then why are the Apostles of Advertising laughing all the way to their off shore bank accounts? The media plays an immense role in shaping the minds of the viewer, as proven by Sesame Street and the like.

With the shift in roles happening at a very rapid rate, and with no accommodations being made for boys and men to evolve as was done for women and girls, boys and men are now at a loss for their usefulness, other then their biological function of siring the next generation. This is not only an unfortunate loss for all of humanity, it is also tragic because it has added yet another source of fuel for misogyny.

Brothers, if we want a better world for our boys and men we must help them to develop all parts of being human, not just the two given precedence for thousands of years; namely, the physical and the academic intellect. Our boys are just as worthy of being nurtured to become more balanced, compassionate, healthful adults. The women of today, and our daughters of tomorrow will no longer accept half developed humans as mates; we want equals, not superiors or inferiors. Yes, we do need protection with your strong arms. But, exactly who or what is it from which we need protecting? Shameful answer, is it not?

We like to believe Western Minded women are a little more emancipated than their sisters elsewhere, and are proud of the successes our women have achieved in the work force, in politics, and any other endeavor they care to take on. At what price have we achieved this? Western Minded men have the advantage of having fairly well schooled mates who have paying work outside the home, contributing substantially to the household budget, thus relieving our men of the full traditional burden of being the sole breadwinner. However, this has not translated into men sharing the traditional burdens of women. Oh yes we are emancipated! Now we are free to work outside the home for money, carry the full burden of the household, perform, or arrange for, all the childcare, and die untimely deaths of the stress related inflictions caused by carrying unduly large loads.

There are men who take on half of the load, they are rare and deserve to be acknowledged for having grown up. However, most do not carry their own weight and are just one more burden for the already worn out female workhorse. Effective, good parenting, childrearing and household management are the hardest jobs there are. Is that why men absent themselves from these for the most part? Good parenting means complete and utter responsibility for the wellbeing of a precious child, preparing it for a happy and productive life by being balanced in all four parts of being human. Is there any other job that comes close to this in terms of significance in ensuring the long-term survival of the species? And that, after all, really is all we are here to do

Brothers, we have relieved some of your burden. When will you grow up and relieve some of ours?

We may like to believe we are different from all other species and do not behave out of instinct. The only difference is that we are just about the youngest known species, hence our adolescent arrogance of our intelligence and importance, and our belief in an infinite supply for our wants. And, we are the only species that behaves in a manner identical to that of the A.I.D.S. virus, invading and consuming its host to death. Other than those charming qualities, we instinctively do just what every other species does; we are born, we grow, we consume energy, we eliminate waste, we reproduce, we age, we die. And every thing we do is done to further one or more of those instinctive ends.

Following inborn instincts the males of all species attempt to dominate in order to secure enough territory and resources to interest a mate with whom to produce offspring, and perpetuate the species. Human males have replaced the territorial aspect with power through amassing money. And, now females are able to do that for themselves in ever increasing numbers. Being a real man today, as defined by the right winged, fundamentalist, corporate, neo-conservative agenda, may be beneficial in impressing other men of the same ilk. However, it fails to garner the interest of a substantive mate with whom to perpetuate the species. And, perhaps that would be a blessing facilitating only the substantial members of the species to reproduce. If the intent is to impress other men, and women of little substance, then pay no heed to this author's words. If, on the other hand, men and boys are to become indispensable members of the entire human family, then it would do the entire living biosphere much good for both boys and men to learn to live as if life really matters, and develop all four aspects of being human.

So what can we do to help create an indispensable role for boys and men once again? Firstly, boys and men have always been indispensable; they have simply chosen to absent themselves from essential roles, thereby appearing to become redundant, and dispensable. Secondly, it would benefit them to learn about ecological feminism and assess where their individual complicity lays in the injustices addressed in this movement (it is about all the major world issues, not about burning bras and male bashing). Thirdly, they need to read this book again, implement all the suggestions, and examine their own lives to determine where they have failed humanity. Fourthly, just fix it, because it is very broken!

If you have a mother, sister, aunt, niece, or other female relative or friend you love, then show it. Become the kind of man they can respect and find indispensable in their lives. If you have a daughter you love, show it. Become the kind of man you would wish for her to have as her equal partner in life. If you have a son you love, show it. Become the kind of man he would be proud to emulate and call his hero.

CHAPTER 12:

BY AGE

If there is to be peace in the world,
There must be peace in the nations.
If there is to be peace in the nations,
There must be peace in the cities.
If there is to be peace in the cities,
There must be peace between neighbours.
If there is to be peace between neighbours,
There must be peace in the home.
If there is to be peace in the home,
There must be peace in the heart.
Lao-Tse

This section has been written with children/youth and seniors/ elders in mind, and does not imply that this is all that would be of benefit to these groups. It is the hope that this entire work would be read by, and be of use, to all groups. However, there are certain ideas the author would prefer to present to different collectives, as these ideas appear to be more applicable to them.

CHILDREN AND YOUTH

The world we have created for our children and youth is very different from what our parents and grandparents had left for us. The rate of change has been much too rapid for human adaptation in a sane and healthy way. We have created a lot of messes, in every part of the planet, and even laid waste the sky and outer space. The good news, dear young ones, is that my generation will all die off in a couple of decades, and will not have to live a full lifetime with the messes. However, the bad news is that we leave you, the next generations, to deal with the messes we were too lazy, too uncaring, too materialistic, too self-absorbed, and too immature to clean up.

It is no longer a matter of laying blame. It is now a matter of doing something about all the messes before they do us in. The bulk of this work thus far has focused on things people of all ages could do to make a difference. The following are a few things children and youth can do to help make the world a better place for all. The young are naturally good, compassionate, and creative. We school all these good attributes right out of them. Following these suggestions might get them on the road to recovering from schooling and becoming truly educated good global citizens.

Dear children and youth,

1   You need to expect your parents to be good parents for you: to give you their time, not more "stuff"; to say "No" to all that is harmful for you; to teach you the skills you need to be a good member of your society; to show their love with their actions, not just with their words or money.

2   And also *you* need to be a good child for your parents: be respectful, mindful and courteous to your family; carry your own weight at home (do your share of chores joyfully); do your best to get educated; spend regular time with your family elders to learn from them; spend more time with humans, and less with machines.

3   Exercise your need and ask your parents for real food and drinks to show they are really serious about your health and happiness.

4   Refuse to wear or own name brands that not only make you into an unpaid billboard, but also they cost your parents far too much money and time to earn the money, and are made by child slaves in poor countries.

5   Do something daily to make the world a better place; smile more, help someone, volunteer, ...

6   Regularly learn something new and useful that you were not told to learn; about the lives of children who made a difference, a new skill, a new idea, ...

7   Pay attention to current events because everything that happens in the world has an effect on your life, and everything you do has an effect on the lives of every living thing.

8   DO NOT believe anything if it does not feel right in your gut, check it out yourself by using several different sources to get your information. The Internet is O.K., your public library and helpful librarians are better sources.

9   Practice good thoughts, good words, and good actions, in dealing with all living things, human or not.

10   Most importantly of all, demand to be taught by parents and

teachers how to live a balanced life through development of all four parts of being human equally; the body, the thinker, the feeler, and the soul.

11 Make sure you have become balanced in all four parts of being human before you even think about becoming a parent.

12 When you do become a parent be one that nurtures all parts of being human and gives of themselves most.

These few things will help you become a better person and that is the main purpose of childhood. Only the human species has such a long period of dependency in childhood. It is meant for you to **LEARN TO BE THE BEST THAT YOU CAN BE.** I know that is going to be hard to do given that a lot of the adults in this world have made little effort to model that for you. For that I am truly sorry.

Begin now to become the kind of person your grandchildren would be proud to call their hero, because you did the right thing just for the sake of doing the right thing, and so made this planet into a safe and healthy place for everything that lives here., now and for seven generations to come.

SENIORS/ ELDERS

There was a time when more people lived more meaningful lives than we seem to now, and they felt they were of use to their families and communities. With the onset of our age of materialism, fewer people feel satisfied that their lives have had meaning, and go to extremes to try to prolong the end, in the hope of finding meaning and purpose for their existence before the inevitable end. (It is very unlikely that those facing the plastic surgeon's scalpel are consciously pondering this insight.) Also, the media plays a significant role in perpetuating the loathing for old age. Until fairly recent times we honored our elders in many ways, the aging body was not abhorred.

To the Western Minded old age is to be kept at bay, as evidenced by the plethora of new products and services introduced daily to ward off the evils of old age. One might wonder at this point in the book, if being female is unacceptable in every aspect, and being a senior is unacceptable, and children are only worthy of being raised by corporations, then what is left of being a human that is acceptable, and not in need of serious modification through the use of products and services supplied by some billion dollar corporation?

This is most unfortunate, for the very people who gave us life and worked hard all their lives for us, are the very ones we now hold as models of what we never want to be. Our seniors and elders need to be productive for as long they choose, and are able. Being active and productive is the best antidote to aging and ill health, along with good nutrition, exercise and attitude. They have knowledge and experience of so much that would help us solve some of the horrendous problems we have created. Most still remember what self-sufficiency meant, and how to acquire it; self-sufficiency leads to greater personal security, a rise in self esteem, and an accompanying decline in behaviours and attitudes that are harmful to Life.

With great humility this author finds she has very little advice to offer our seniors/elders; it is they that we need to be advising us. And so, with all due respect the following are offered for the consideration of our seniors and elders.

1   Exercise your physical and mental faculties daily.

2   Spend time outdoors frequently.

3   Talk to your grandchildren about how to live simply.

4   Keep a positive, joyful attitude.

5   Remain independent as long as it is safe for you to do so.

6   Accept the inevitable aging with grace and dignity.

7   You will always have the right to tell off your children if they are wreaking havoc in the world, or not being effective parents. So, use it! You have earned the right!

8   Remember, the young have only youth, whereas you have experienced all the ages, had a lifetime full of experience, adventure, love, learning, contribution, associations, and there are many individuals in the world right now who are carrying your genes into the future of the human race.

If you are able to keep well, and try to follow some of the advice given above and in previous pages, you will make a very big difference in the future wellbeing of your descendants.

CHAPTER 13:

IN THE END

I was not aware of the moment when I crossed the threshold of this life.
What was the power that made me open out into this vast mystery like a
Bud in the forest at midnight!
When in the morning I looked upon the light I felt in a moment that I was
No stranger in this world, that the inscrutable without name and Form had
taken me in its arms in the form of my own mother.
Even so, in death the same unknown will appear as ever known to me. And,
Because I love this life, I know I shall love death as well.
The child cries out when from the right breast the mother takes it away,
In the very next moment to find in the left it's consolation.

Robindernath Tagore

PART ONE: THE PHYSICAL END

This chapter is not only about the end of this book, but also it is about the end of one's current life, about an ultimate end. "There is a season to everything" as Ecclesiastes stated in his Desiderata, and humans are not exempt from this. We share the sequences of our lifecycle with every thing that exists, whether universes, galaxies, stars, plants, or non-human animals; we come into existence from nowhere, grow, reproduce, and vanish into somewhere. The physical form of everything can be seen to transform itself after death into constituents that nourish the gestation and birth of some other physical entity. Matter and energy are one, conserved and transformed, as they nurture Life to renew its self. All Life nurtures new Life's evolution.

Not so for the Western Minded! We place our deceased bodily remains in nuclear blast proof containers to remain, forever, apart from our physical source. Perhaps this is a blessing, since the bodily remains of most of the Western Minded contain a storehouse of toxins accumulated over a lifetime, offering little or no organic hummus to push up daisies.

The very earliest ideas about burials involved returning the body to the womb of mother Earth to be reborn. Later, for the Greeks, "koimeteria" was a Place of The Mother where the dead could rest as closely as possible to the temples of the Goddess. This practice was later adopted by various churches by placing cemeteries beside church buildings, along with the practice of preserving the body as earlier royalty had done. Ancient royalty often claimed divine heritage, had the wealth and labour to build eternal monuments for it's bodies, and so was buried with the view to maintaining the body for all eternity. Unfortunately, the idea eventually began to appeal to the emerging wealthy and powerful as a status symbol, and then trickled down to the masses who blindly emulate the wealthy and powerful.

The practice of this custom would seem logical given that the Western Minded, having lived a life of disengagement from the non-human part of nature, would continue to do so in death. There is also an element of deeply hidden misogyny in this custom. If the origins of burials lie in the return to the womb of the Goddess, then it would also seem logical to prevent all contact with Her upon death, since Her femaleness is feared and loathed. There is too an element of regret in this custom; regret of a life unsatisfied and in need of solace by having at least the body continue to exist a little longer. And lastly, in our times of worship of the God of Consumer Goods, the custom is now a multi-billion dollar industry, promoted by the Apostles of Advertising.

The health authorities would have us believe it is for health reasons that bodies must be in sealed coffins. Rather hypocritical, given that they are the same ones who give approval to all the allopathic drugs that kill hundreds of thousands yearly, and will not approve naturopathic remedies that rarely kill anyone. With well meaning intentions, a limited schooling, and little understanding of the big picture of what it means to be human, our leaders, officials and authorities have misguided us into the belief that the body must not contact the Earth or Cosmos once Life has left it. Poppycock!

We deny life to so much more than ourselves with this custom; decaying bodies in tanker coffins occupy valuable land, in some of the most scenic locations of this world, and serve absolutely no useful purpose to Life. It is our spiritual responsibility to be as connected to Life in death as are all the other manifestations of Life; especially all the other creatures, our elders, amongst whom we are the youngest species on Earth. When we begin to learn, love and live as if Life really matters, when we learn to approach aging and death with the same joy as we approach a new born life, then we will be worthy of sharing this planet with other creature elders, then we will have matured into a species worthy of having Life.

PART TWO: THE END OF THIS WORK

Dear Reader,

This work is only the first of a number of books inspired while undergoing cancer treatment and recovery. The experience has been of such profound intensity, and spiritual inspiration, that I feel I would be remiss in not sharing with the world the insights that have percolated to the top of my consciousness. This work has been written with the purest of intentions to make the world a better place for all of Life, in particular for the children.

The intent has been to raise awareness of individual complicity in the big global problems and to offer simple solutions that would address the great wrongs we, the Western Minded, perpetrate on all the innocents of this world. Not one amongst us has the right to eat, drink, purchase or discard anything as we wish. Every good and thoughtful act we commit has positive global consequences. Every bad and selfish act we commit has negative global consequences. Few amongst us are able to live with the purity that Gandhi ji had tried to do. However, each of us is able to make every one of the changes recommended. That is, if we are not lazy.

The oft seen quote, **"LIVE SIMPLY SO OTHERS MAY SIMPLY LIVE"**, should no longer need any explanation, and the need for adopting it as ones major goal should be obvious. We can dream a new dream of a world where:

1. Children are made the #1 priority.

2. Parenting is given the highest status of all vocations.

3. Spirituality takes precedence over religion; exhausting the exploration of the inner landscape before any further space exploration.

4. All schooling institutions are transformed to Educational institutions and all education is free, as is now available in some of the poorest countries, such as Cuba.

5. Smaller, self-contained green communities are the future norm for development.

6. Organic, whole foods and drinks are available to all at affordable prices.

7. First class universal health care is a reality for everyone in the world, as are any other social services, as required.

8. The circumstances giving rise to the need for weapons are eliminated; all military personnel spend at least six months of working on organic farms as part of their peace making training; and the purpose of the military to become one of doing seva for all of humanity.

9. The need for governments, policing and the judicial systems is diminished because humans are taking responsibility through developing their own internal locus of control.

If we can dream this kind of a world then we can make it real. We have the potential to grow up into a noble species that brought itself, and much in the biosphere, back from brutal extinction, restoring the entire planet to its gloriously vibrant state.

If you have stayed with me this far I thank you for the privilege
of sharing your precious moments with my thoughts.

If you have been offended, choose not to be; none was intended.
If you have been enraged, reflect on the real cause.
If you have been shamed, make amends.
If you have been disillusioned, search for other inspiration.
If you have been amused, share the joy with the world.
If you have been inspired, please act on it.
If you have been educated, pass on the message.
If you have been empowered, use it for Life.

Wishing you a meaningful life with good health and happiness,
Your companion in search of answers,
Pummy Kaur

**"ONCE YOU MAKE A DECISION THE UNIVERSE
CONSPIRES TO MAKE IT HAPPEN".**
Ralph Waldo Emerson

AFTERWORD

"I am only one,
But still I am one.
I cannot do everything,
But still I can do something.
And because I cannot do everything
I will not refuse to do the
Something that I can do."
                              Edward Everett Hale

If the urgency for individual change has not been stressed enough then, hopefully, the following summary will inspire more action immediately.

~ We are depleting limited supplies of fossil fuels very rapidly, and control of these is the main reason for current wars where thousands of innocent civilians die.

~ For countries like Canada climate change is adding a new dimension to sovereignty issues as the northern ice melts, revealing resource rich islands to which other countries are laying claim, creating more tension and conflict in the world.

~ We are converting all natural resources into toxins, making the biosphere and all of life in it very sick, especially our children and vulnerable elderly parents.

~ All of our processes for converting non-human nature into toxic waste (processed foods and drinks, disposables, synthetics, toiletries, cosmetics, cleansers, gadgets, "stuff") deplete natural resources, create environmental pollution, add to global warming and climate change, and have disastrous effects on every living thing, especially the biosphere.

~ It is over the control of all our limited resources that war is waged on this planet, and why we have nuclear weapon amassment in sufficient quantity to obliterate all trace of Life as we know, and as we need it to be for our survival.

~ We are depleting fresh water faster than the Earth's systems are able to replenish it, as is the case with nearly every other natural resource that we are depleting during all the manufacturing of "stuff", and the disposal of all our waste "stuff".

~ Millions of people in the Majority World have their basic rights for survival, and fundamental human rights, violated

continuously by the selfish actions of the lazy Western Minded people in order to consume more "stuff".

~ Poor parenting continues to produce increasing numbers of
insecure children who become insecure adults, who further
add to human inflicted misery on the many innocents, where
ever the Western Minded are able to infect cultures worldwide.

~ Few people are educated, and too many are schooled, producing wave after wave of dysfunctional, self-absorbed adults.

~ Too much of the global media is in the control of too few,
producing unthinking, uncaring monoculture everywhere.

~ Multinational corporations have too much control over the
lives of everyone, they have more rights than nations of people, and even more than the only living biosphere in which
humans can survive.

~ The quality of the soil in which food is grown is already
too low to support a planet full of reasonably healthy people.

~ The natural systems of our life sustaining biosphere have just
about reached their limits to self correct, and will soon eliminate us like an undesirable virus, for we are not genetically
programmed to survive in the kind of biosphere that our
greed, laziness, and selfishness are creating.

Many would consider anyone who now fails to act responsibly to
be either a sociopath or just stupid. If one is ignorant, unaware of
one's complicity in global problems, then, perhaps one has a limited excuse. However, those that know better, who have choices,
and consistently choose to act irresponsibly are simply an immature, lazy, evil plague on humanity and its only home. (No,
Gandhi ji would not approve of these words, but they need to be
said, because they speak an uncomfortable truth.)

The life of Gandhi ji is a source of inspiration to many around the world, and will continue to be. He was not a perfect man; in fact he was a somewhat negligent parent. He was, however, a model of devotion to the highest ideals of being a responsible part of the Cosmos. He struggled daily with living up to the exceptionally high standards he had set for himself. Gandhi ji is one of the few humans believed to have achieved the highest, the fifth level of Abraham Maslow's hierarchy of human needs, that of self actualization. Most of us of the Western Minded Minority World are struggling around the second and third levels, while too much of the Majority world struggles at the first level. If it was hard for Gandhi ji to live up to his ideals, imagine how much harder it is for the rest of us.

Please do not give up in despair or guilt at the enormity of the problems. We created them, and **WE CAN, WE MUST** solve them. We have allowed them into existence with our acts of complicity, by commission and omission. Knowing the links now between our individual actions and global problems ought to move us away from our lazy self-centeredness to thoughtful, actively healthful life styles, which nurture peace, security, and abundance for all who share our only biosphere. It has always been entirely up to us to shape humanity, as we would wish it to be. Now, with instant communication, there is no longer any excuse for the Western Minded to remain conveniently ignorant of our part in global problems, other than the ultimate sin of being too lazy to care about anything beyond our own noses.

The challenge is there before us. Do we have the ovaries and the balls to accept it?

At this point a further request is made of the readers to help strengthen the messages of this work, and to help the author further her own progress into being a more responsible keeper of her global siblings. Please log on to the web site

www.WhatWouldGandhiDo.ca

and add your solutions to global issues, showing the links between what your personal action(s) have been and the global issues they have addressed. They will be monitored for appropriate content and language at the discretion of the Web Manager.

Or you may write to:
    W.W.G.D.?
    Hillcrest P.O.B. 71522,
    White Rock,
    British Columbia,
    Canada,
    V4B 5J5

All constructive contribution would be very welcome. If you have destructive contribution, please don't fill my cyberspace or mailbox with them. This work was written with the best of intentions to make life better for ALL, and only positive, constructive contributions can further that end. All destructive contributions require their authors to self reflect first, and then find constructive ways to offer them.

"It is very difficult to shake hands with a clenched fist,"
Indira Gandhi.

SOURCES OF INSPIRATION AND INFLUENCE

A   PEOPLE:

1   Aung San Sui Kyi, Sophia Lyon Fahs, Vandana Shiva, Arundathi Roy, Reanne Eisler, Mary-Wyn Ashford, Hulda Roddan, Quan Yin, Maude Barlow, The Raging Grannies, Gro Brundtland, Malai Joya

2   Mohandas K. Gandhi, His Holiness the Dalai Lama, Stephen Lewis, Fidel Castro, Nelson Mandela, Tommy Douglas, Pierre Burton, Hugo Chavez, Subcommandante Marcos

3   The Mothers of the Disappeared, Women In Black, Tibetan peace activists, Falun Dafa practitioners in China, all the groups and individuals who continue to fight for the rights of those who can not do it for themselves.

B   VISUAL/VIDEO

1   Burke, J., After the Warming, Parts 1 and 2, 1990
2   Zoned For Slavery
3   Mickey Mouse Goes To Haiti
4   Moore, M., Bowling for Columbine, 2003
5   Robbins, J., Diet For A Small Planet, 1994
6   C.B.C. television, and Newsworld
7   C.T.V. Newsnet
8   B.B.C. World News
9   A.B.C. (Australian Broad Casting)

C   ELECTRONIC

1   www.newint.org
2   www.policyalternatives.ca
3   www.CouncilOfCanadians.ca
4   www.cbc.ca
5   www.AmnestyInternational.ca
6   www.adbusters.ca

7   www.livingvalues.org
8   www.page.bc.ca

D   AUDIO

C.B.C. Radio One, Two, Three and short wave

E   PRINT

1. Adams, C. J., <u>Ecofeminism and the Sacred</u>, Continuum, N.Y., 1993
2. Ainger, K., et al ed., <u>The New Internationalist Journals</u>, 1986-2006
3. Alibek, K., <u>Biohazard</u>, Random House, 1999
4. Anton, D., <u>Diversity, Globalization and the Ways of Nature</u>, International Development Research Center, Ottawa, 1995
5. Araya, V., <u>The God of the Poor</u>, Orbis, New York, 1987
6. Armstrong, K., <u>The Gospel According to Woman</u>, Doubleday, New York, 1986
7. Ashford, M-W., <u>Enough Blood Shed</u>, New Society Publisher, B.C., 2006
8. Axworthy, L., <u>Navigating the New World</u>, Vintage Canada, Toronto, 2004
9. Babcock, C., ed., <u>Walk Quietly The Beautiful Trail</u>, Hallmark, Kansan, 1973
10. Baird, V., <u>The No-Nonsense Guide to Sexual Diversity</u>, Verso, London, 2002
11. Bakan, J., <u>The Corporation</u>, Penguin, Toronto, 2004
12. Bales, K., <u>Disposable People: New Slavery in the Global Economy</u>, University of California Press, California, 1999
13. Barbour, I. G., <u>Issues In Science And Religion</u>, Harper, N.Y., 1966
14. Barbour, I. G., <u>Religion In An Age of Science</u>, Harper, San Francisco, 1990

15. Barney, G., <u>Threshold 2000; Critical Issues and Spiritual Values for a Global Age</u>, Millennium Institute, Virginia, 1999

16. Barstow, A. J., <u>Withcraze,</u> Pandora, San Francisco, 1994

17. Berger, J., <u>The Gaia Atlas of First Peoples</u>, Anchor Books, Sydney, 1990

18. Bernstein, P., <u>The Power of Gold</u>, John Wiley and Sons, New York, 2000

19. Black, M., <u>The NO-Nonsense Guide to International Trade</u>, Verso, London,2002

20. Blix, H., <u>Disarming Iraq</u>, Bloomsberry, London, 2004

21. Blum Wm., <u>Rogue State</u>, Common Courage Press, Maine, 2000

22. Bohm, D., Peat, D. F., <u>Science, Order and Creativity</u>, Rutledge, London, 2000

23. Braybrook, M., <u>Stepping Stones to a Global Ethic</u>, S.C.M. Press, London, 1992

24. Brazier, C., <u>The NO-Nonsense Guide to World History</u>, Verso, London, 2002

25. Brown, L., et al., <u>State of The World</u>, W.W. Norton, New York, 2005

26. Burrows, G., <u>The No-Nonsense Guide to The Arms Trade</u>, Verso, London, 2002

27. Buzan, T., <u>Use Both Sides of Your Brain,</u> Dutton New, York, 1974

28. Brundtland, G., et al., <u>Our Common Future</u>, Oxford University Press, 1987

29. Cajete, G., <u>Look to the Mountain: An Ecology of Indigenous Education</u>, Kivavi Press, Colorado, 1994

30. Caldicott, H., <u>If You Love This Planet</u>, W.W. Norton, New York, 1992

31. Campbell, J., <u>The Power of Myth</u>, Doubleday, N.Y., 1988

32. Capra, F., <u>The Turning Point</u>, Simon & Shuster, New

York, 1977

33. Caulfield, C., Masters of Illusions: The World Bank and the Poverty of Nations, Henry Holt, New York 1996

34. Chaudry, H., The Evolution of Integral Consciousness, Quest, Madras, 1997

35. Chomsky, N., Rogue States, South End Press, Cambridge, 2000

36. Chomsky, N., 9-11, Seven Stories Press, New York, 2002

37. Clark, B., Growing Up Gifted, Charles E. Merrill, Columbus, 1983

38. Dalglish, P., The Courage of Children: My Life with the World's Poorest Kids, Harper Collins, 1998

39. Davies, P., The Mind Of God, Simon & Shuster, New York, 1992

40. Dossey, L., Space, Time and Medicine, Shambhala, Boston, 1985

41. Dyer, G., Future Tense: The Coming World Order, M&S, Toronto, 2004

42. Duke, J., The Green Pharmacy, St. Martin's Press, U.S.A., 1998

43. Easwaran, E., Gandhi: The Man, Nilgiri Press, 1997

44. Eisler, R., The Chalice And the Blade, Harper, San Francisco, 1988

45. Ellmann, R., O'Clair, R., eds., Modern Poems, Norton & Co., New York, 1976

46. Ellwood, W., The NO-Nonsense Guide to Globalization, Verso, London, 2002

47. Ferguson, N., Empire, Penguin Books, London, 2003

48. Fischer, L., ed., The Essential Gandhi, Vintage Books, New York, 1990

49. Flannery, T., The Future Eaters, Reed New Holland, Australia, 2002

50. Fone, B., Homophobia, Henry Holt, New York,

2000

51. Fonseca, I., <u>Bury Me Standing: The Gypsies and their Journey</u>, Vintage, N.Y., 1996

52. Freire, P., <u>Pedagogy of the Oppressed</u>, Continuum, New York, 1995

53. Gandhi, M.K., <u>The Way to God</u>, Beverly Hills Books, 1999

54. Gandhi, M.K., <u>Vows And Observances</u>, Beverly Hills Books, 1999

55. Gardner, H., <u>Frames of Mind</u>, Basic Books,, 1989

56. Gatto, J., <u>Dumbing Us Down: The Hidden Curriculum of Compulsory Schooling</u>, New Society Publishers, B.C., 1992

57. Gibran, K., <u>The Prophet</u>, Knopf, New York, 1992

58. Glieck, J., <u>Chaos: The Making of a New Science</u>, Penguin, New York, 1998

59. Gleick, J., <u>FSTR</u>, Random House, New York, 2000

60. Godrej, D., <u>The No-Nonsense Guide to Climate Change</u>, Verso, London, 2002

61. Goertzel, V., Goertzel, M., <u>Cradles of Eminence</u>, Little, Brown & Company, Boston, 1962

62. Groff, S., <u>Beyond the Brain</u>, State University of New York Press, New York, 1985

63. Guevara, C., <u>Global Justice</u>, Ocean Press, Australia, 2002

64. Gurrian, M., <u>The Wonder of Boys</u>, Penguin Putnam, New York, 1996

65. Hahn, Thich Nhat, <u>Being Peace</u>, Parallax Press, California, 1987

66. Hamilton, J., <u>Entangling Alliances: How the Third World Shapes our Lives</u>, Seven Locks Press, Washington, 1990

67. Hamilton, J., <u>Main Street America and The Third World</u>, Seven Locks Press, Washington, 1988

68. Hampden-Turner, C., <u>The Seven Cultures of Capitalism</u>, Doubleday, New York, 1993

69. Harcourt, V., <u>In The Beginning</u>, Janovich, San Francisco, 1987

70. Harrid. S., <u>Two Way Aboriginal Schooling: Education and Cultural Survival</u>, Aboriginal, Studies Press, Canberra, 1990

71. Hartmann, T., <u>The Last Hours of Ancient Sunlight</u>, Harmony Books, New York, 1996

72. Hawking, S., <u>Black Holes and Baby Universes and Other Essays</u>, Bantam, N. Y., 1993

73. Hawking, S., <u>A Brief History of Time</u>, Bantam, New York, 1996

74. Hawking, S., <u>The Universe In A Nutshell</u>, Bantam, New York, 1998

75. Heinberg, R., <u>Cloning The Buddha</u>, Quest Books, India, 1999

76. Henley, T., <u>Rediscovery: Ancient Pathways</u>, New Direction, W.C.W. Committee, Canada, 1989

77. Horowitz, L., <u>Emerging Virus: A.I.D.S. and Ebola, Nature, Accident, or Intentional</u>, Tetrahedron Inc., Massachusetts, 1997

78. Hughes, L., <u>The NO-Nonsense Guide to Indigenous Peoples</u>, Verso, London, 2002

79. Instituo Del Tercer Mundo, <u>The World Guide, New Internationalist,</u> Oxford, 1999

80. Kakar, S., <u>Shamans, Mystics, and Doctors</u>, University of Chicago Press, Chicago, 1991

81. Kaur, H., <u>Global Education: A Movement And Methodology</u>, unpublished, 1994

82. Klein, N., <u>NO LOGO</u>, A. Knoff, Canada, 2000

83. Liebes, S., Sahtouris, E., Swimme, B., <u>A Walk Through Time: From Stardust to Us</u>, Wiley and Sons, New York, 1998

84. Lindqvist, S., <u>Exterminate The Brutes</u>, New Press, New York, 1996

85. Lovelock, J., <u>The Ages of Gaia</u>, W.W. Norton, New York, 1988

86. Mazis, G. A., <u>The Trickster, Magician and Grieving Man; Reconecting Men with the Earth</u>, Bear and Company, New York, 1994

87. Marber, I., Edgson, V., <u>The Food Doctor,</u> Collins & Brown, London, 2004

88. McCaughrean, G., <u>Myths And Legends of the World,</u> Orion, London 1997

89. McFague, S., <u>The Body of God</u>, Fortress Press, Minneapolis, 1993

90. Merchant, C. ed., <u>Ecology: Key Concepts in Critical Theory</u>, Humanities Press, New Jersey, 1994

91. Mandela, N., <u>Long Walk To Freedom,</u> Abacus, London, 1997

92. Marti, J., <u>Writings on the Americas</u>, Ocean Press, Melbourne, 1999

93. Montague, A., <u>The Natural Superiority of Women</u>, Collier, New York, 1992

94. Morgan, P., Braybrook, M., <u>Testing The Global Ethic</u>, CoNexus Press, MI, 1998

95. Morris, R., <u>The Nature of Reality</u>, Noonday, New York, 1988

96. Musafir, G., <u>Selected Poems</u>, Shobhna, New Delhi, 1969

97. Neihardt, J., <u>Black Elk Speaks</u>, University of Nebraska Press, U.S., 1997

98. O'Murchu, D., <u>Quantum Theology</u>, Crossroads, New York, 1998

99. Pagels, E., <u>The Gnostic Gospels</u>, Vintage Books, N.Y., 1989

100. Pawlick, T., <u>The End of Food</u>, Greystone, Vancouver, 2006

101. Peck, S. M., <u>People of the Lie</u>, Touchstone, New York, 1978

102. Peck, S. M., <u>The Different Drum</u>, Touchstone, New York, 1987

103. Peck, S. M., <u>The Road Less Traveled</u>, Touchstone,

New York, 1983

104. Pedreson, L. E., <u>Dark Hearts: The Unconscious Forces that Shape Men's Lives</u>, Shambhala, Boston, 1991

105. Pelletier, K. R., <u>Towards a Science of Consciousness</u>, Celestial Arts, California, 1985

106. Penrose, R., <u>Shadows of the Mind</u>, Oxford University Press, Oxford, 1994

107. Peter-Ross, E., <u>Biodemocracy</u>, Royal Tern, Cape Town, 1999

108. Pike, G., Shelby, D., <u>Global Teacher, Global Learner</u>, Hodder & Stoughton, Kent, 1988

109. Pilger, J., <u>The New Rulers of the World</u>, Verso, London, 2003

110. Porter, R., ed., <u>Medicine: A History of Healing</u>, Marlow & Co., 1997

111. Ransom, D., <u>The No-Nonsense Guide to Fair Trade</u>, Verso, London, 2003

112. Ravindra, R., <u>Science And Spirit</u>, Paragon, New York, 1990

113. Reuther, R. R., <u>Gaia & God</u>, Harper, San Francisco, 1992

114. Robbins, J., <u>Diet For A New America</u>, Fithzhenry & Whiteside, Toronto, 1987_

115. Roche, D., <u>Building Global Security</u>, N.C. Press, Toronto, 1989

116. Ruhe, P., <u>Gandhi</u>, Phaidon Press, New York, 2001

117. Rumi, <u>The Glance: Songs of Soul-Meeting</u>, Penguin, New York, 1999

118. Sagan, C., <u>Cosmos</u>,

119. Sagan, C., <u>The Dragons of Eden</u>, Ballantine, New York, 1977

120. Schlosser, E., <u>Fast Food Nation</u>, Harper Collins, New York, 2001

121. Seabrook, J., <u>The No-Nonsense Guide to Class, Caste, & Hierarchies</u>, Verso, London, 2002

122. Shiva, V., <u>Biopiracy</u>, South End Press, Boston, 1997

123. Shiva, V., <u>Water Wars, Between The Lines</u>, Toronto, 1997

124. Sinclair, S., <u>G.A.T.S.: How the World Trade Organization's new "services" Negotiations threaten democracy</u>, C.C.P.A., Ottawa, 2000

125. Smith, H., <u>World's Religions</u>, Harper, San Francisco, 1994

126. Smolan, R., Moffitt, P., Naythons, M., <u>The Power to Heal: Ancient Arts and Modern Medicine</u>, Princeton Hall, Toronto, 1990

127. Swanson, J., <u>Poor-Bashing, Between The Lines</u>, Toronto, 2001

128. Spong, J., <u>Why Christianity Must Change or Die</u>, Harper Collins, San Francisco, 1998

129. Stalker, P., <u>The No-Nonsense Guide to International Migration</u>, Verso, London, 2002

130. Sweet, L., <u>God In The Classroom</u>, Mclelland & Stewartt, Toronto, 1997

131. Swift, R., <u>The No-Nonsense Guide to Democracy</u>, Verso, London, 2002

132. Tagore, R., <u>Gitanjali</u>, Schribner, New York, 1997

133. Unitarian Universalist Association, <u>Singing The Living Tradition</u>, Boston Press, Boston, 1993

134. Velikovsky, I., <u>Earth In Upheaval</u>, Del, New York, 1974

135. Viola, H.J., <u>After Columbus</u>, Orion Books, New York, 1990

136. Walker, B., <u>The Women's Encyclopedia of Myths and Secrets</u>, Harper And Row, San Francisco, 1983

137. Watts, A., <u>Beyond Theology; The Art of Godmanship</u>, Vintage, New York, 1974

138. Wilber, K., <u>Spectrum of Consciousness,</u> Quest Books, Madras, 1993

139. Wilber, K., ed., <u>Quantum Questions</u>, Shambhala, Boston, 2003

140. Wills, G., <u>Papal Sin</u>, Doubleday, Toronto, 2000
141. Zukav, G., <u>The Dancing Wu Li Masters</u>, Bantam, New York, 1979